THE NEPAL COOKBOOK

THE NEPAL COOKBOOK

ASSOCIATION OF NEPALIS IN THE AMERICAS

Illustrations by
PALDEN CHOEDAK OSHOE

Snow Lion Publications
Ithaca, New York

Snow Lion Publications
P. O. Box 6483
Ithaca, NY 14851
607-273-8519

ISBN 1-55939-060-3

Library of Congress Cataloging-in-Publication Data

The Nepal Cookbook / Association of Nepalis in the Americas.
    p. cm.
  ISBN 1-55939-060-3
  1. Cookery, Nepali. I. Association of Nepalis in the Americas.
TX724.5.N4N43 1996
641.595496--dc20

TABLE OF CONTENTS

The Purpose of the Association of Nepalis in the Americas   6
Preface   7
Special Ingredients   9

Snacks and Appetizers   15
Soups and Lentils   31
Vegetables   43
Meat, Chicken, and Seafood   69
Chutneys and Pickles   93
Rice and Breads   119
Desserts   131

English-Nepali Glossary   159
The Contributors   163

THE PURPOSE OF THE ASSOCIATION OF NEPALIS IN THE AMERICAS

The Association of Nepalis in the Americas promotes preservation of Nepali identity and culture in the Americas, fosters cordial relations among Nepalis and Americans, and encourages the effective participation of Nepali Americans in the communities in which they live.

Proceeds from the sale of *The Nepal Cookbook* will be used by the Association of Nepalis in the Americas to support educational and charitable projects.

PREFACE

This cookbook is the proud collective project of all the Nepali people who have contributed recipes that were previously part of their family's secret oral treasure and tradition. This important step in the building of a new tradition in the Americas "serves as a first major source of information on Nepali recipes to our future generations," according to Amar Giri, past president of the Association of Nepalis in the Americas. Contributions of recipes came from Nepalis all over North America, as well as those visiting from Kathmandu, and crossed political, association, religious, and ethnic differences. The recipes reflect the diets of both rich and poor, and represent food commonly prepared in the mountains as well as the Tarai plains.

Nepali cuisine was influenced by the early development of Kathmandu Valley into a vibrant cultural center. From the harsh topography of the mountains came *tama* (fermented bamboo shoots) and *gundruk* (fermented dried leafy greens), *sukeko moola* (sun-dried daikon), *sukuti* (dried meat), *maseura* (sun-dried lentil and vegetable balls), *titura* (sun-dried lentil balls), *quantee* (sprouted mixed beans), *machha selo* (dried fish), and *sankkhtra* (dried citrus pickles). As early as the fourth century A.D., spinach and onions were introduced from Nepal to China, and in turn, *tama tusa* (bamboo tips) were brought from China to Nepal. Potatoes, now the staple food of the Sherpas, were introduced from Europe about 200 years ago.

The Nepali diet consists primarily of rice, corn, millet, wheat, and lentils (*dal*) supplemented by leafy greens and other fresh vegetables during the growing season. Meat (*masu*) and fish (*machha*) are used on special occasions and during festivals, although those who can afford it eat meat, fish, and poultry often. During the festival of Dasain, lavish meat dishes are served; during the festival of Tihar, sweets and vegetable dishes abound; during Janai Purnima, *quantee* is essential. Nepali meat curries are unusual in that they often include fresh vegetables (such as cauliflower, turnip, squash, and green garlic). Before the advent of new highways and improved transportation throughout Nepal, fresh vegetables were not readily available during the summer; in these times, sun-dried vegetables, lentil balls, bamboo shoots, dried onions, and root vegetables like *tarul* (yam) and *pindalu* (taro) were generally eaten.

Nepali food, which is simple and subtle in flavor, is influenced by the cuisines of both India and Tibet. Commonly used ingredients are cumin, black pepper, turmeric, red and green chilies, garlic, ginger, onions, and scallions. The main cooking fats are mustard oil, clarified butter (*ghiu*), corn oil, and soybean oil. Most of the ingredients needed are readily available in supermarkets and in many health-food, Asian, and Indian grocery stores. The amounts of various ingredients called for in the recipes should be used as a guide only and can be adjusted according to the taste desired; most of the recipes serve four to six people unless stated otherwise. A typical full-course Nepali meal includes an appetizer, rice, soup or lentils, a vegetable, meat, and a pickle or chutney, followed by dessert and tea, coffee, or other beverage.

Special thanks go to the contributors for all their time and effort in collecting and recording the recipes in this book. The Association of Nepalis in the Americas also wishes to express appreciation to Snow Lion Publications for the care and attention they put into producing *The Nepal Cookbook*.

SPECIAL INGREDIENTS

In the following list, we give descriptions of the special ingredients, spices and cooking methods that are essential for creating authentic Nepali cuisine. Most of these ingredients are readily available in larger supermarkets and Asian groceries.

Asafetida
Hing in Nepali. This is a dried gum resin available in powder or solid form from Indian grocery stores. It is used in minute quantities because it has a very strong flavor.

Black Cumin Seeds
Mungrelo in Nepali. This variety of cumin has smaller seeds than the common variety, with a milder and sweeter smell. The seeds are mostly used whole because of the mellow flavor.

Cardamom
Widely available, cardamom comes in two varieties: black (called *alaichi* in Nepali) and green (*sukumel* in Nepali). The black variety is larger and has black pods. It is used slightly cracked or crushed to get the full flavor in rice dishes. Commercially available ground cardamom is the black variety. The green variety has green pods and is harvested and sun-dried in India. It is used to flavor meat and sweet dishes, and in making *garam masala*.

Chili Powder

Ground, dried red chili. This is *not the same* as the prepared spice mix intended for Mexican-style cooking that is sold as "chili powder" in American supermarkets and contains cumin, garlic, and other spices. Ground red chili is available in Indian groceries and in the specialty sections of some supermarkets.

Chutneys

See Pickles.

Cilantro

Hario dhaniya paat in Nepali; also called Chinese parsley or coriander leaves. This refers to the fresh, tender leaves of the coriander plant, used as a common garnish for chutneys and in cooked dishes. When recipes in this book call for coriander, the mature dried seed of the plant is indicated.

Clarified Butter

Called *ghiu* in Nepali and *ghee* in Hindi, this is available in jars from Indian groceries and many supermarkets. Clarified butter is made by heating the butter slowly and separating the clear oil from the milk solids, which are discarded. To make your own, slowly heat 1 lb. sweet butter in a heavy saucepan over medium-low heat. If you like, add 2 bay leaves to the butter. Simmer gently for 20 minutes. Spoon off the white foam from the surface of the heated butter. Do not stir. Turn the heat off and let the residue settle to the bottom. Pour off the clear liquid from the top into a glass container, and discard the thick residue. Clarified butter may be stored in the refrigerator for up to six months. 1 lb. of solid butter will yield 1 cup of clarified butter.

Curry Powder

A ready-made ground spice mix widely available in supermarkets.

Dal

The Nepali term includes lentils, chickpeas and small beans. These are available in many varieties from Indian groceries and larger supermarkets. Each has a distinctive taste and texture. The more common are: *chana dal*, small chickpeas, split, with the skins removed;

moong dal, also called mung beans or green mung, split, with or without the skins removed; *toor dal*, yellow lentils, also called pigeon peas, split, with the skins removed; *mussoor dal*, orange lentils, split, with the skins removed; and *urad dal*, black lentils, split, with or without the skins removed.

Fennel Seeds
Saunf in Nepali; they resemble cumin seeds and have a slight flavor of licorice. Anise seed can often be substituted for fennel. Fennel seeds are sometimes chewed after a meal as a mouth freshener, like the traditionally served cloves and cardamom.

Fenugreek
Methi in Nepali; it is one of the most important spices used in Nepali cooking. Fenugreek seeds are brownish-yellow in color. Added to hot oil at the beginning of cooking, the seeds are cooked until they turn dark brown in color.

Garam Masala
Ground, mixed spices, widely available commercially under this name. Home-made *garam masala* is fresher and more flavorful than the commercial preparations.

To make your own, dry-roast the following whole spices separately until fragrant:

5 tbsp coriander seeds	2 tsp ground cinnamon
3 tbsp cumin seeds	1 tsp whole cloves
1 tbsp black peppercorns	1 tsp ground nutmeg
2 tsp black cardamom seeds	

Grind the roasted spices into a fine powder in a coffee grinder. Store in an airtight container.

Gundruk
Gundruk is a typical and popular Nepalese vegetable dish prepared from leafy green vegetables that are fermented and then sun-dried (see directions, page 32). It is used in soups (page 32), pickles (page 101), and other dishes.

Jimbu

Dried, aromatic grass from the Himalayan regions. It is sold in strands, and just a small pinch is enough to flavor a dish. This herb cannot be bought in Indian groceries. As a substitute, people sometimes use the roots of bulb garlic, but this does not duplicate the distinctive flavor of *jimbu*.

Lovage Seeds

Jwanu in Nepali, *ajowan* in Hindi. These seeds resemble celery seeds and are closely related to caraway and cumin. The seeds are mostly used whole in Nepali cooking, and are added to hot oil at the beginning to flavor the dish.

Pickles

Achar in Nepali is a highly spiced condiment perfumed with ginger, garlic, and hot chilies, and is considered indispensable to a complete Nepali meal. Sometimes served as a vegetable dish in its own right rather than as a condiment, *achar* may use either raw or cooked vegetables, and it may be preserved or prepared fresh. In this book, "chutney" is used to refer to *achar* having a consistency like a thick sauce, and "pickle" refers to *achar* recipes for spiced vegetables, fruits, meats, etc. in which the main ingredient is in chunks or left whole.

Rice Flakes

Chiura in Nepali is pounded rice, also called flat or beaten rice. There are two types of *chiura* available in Indian grocery stores: thick *chiura*, and very thin *chiura*. Most Nepalese prefer the thick variety because it tastes better and holds up well when it is deep fried or used in other recipes. *Chiura* will keep for more than six months.

Szechwan Pepper

Recipes in this book that call for szchewan pepper are best prepared using *timbur*. Unavailable commercially in this country, *timbur* is the single most important spice used in *achar* (Nepali pickles and chutneys). It is almost always used in ground form.

Tamarind

An acidic pulp from the seed pods of the tamarind tree. Readily available in Indian groceries and larger supermarkets, tamarind comes in a concentrated prepared form as well as in the whole seed pods. To make tamarind pulp from the whole pods, boil the pods in a little water for 5 minutes. Mash the cooled tamarind with a fork to release a pulpy paste. Strain the paste through a cheesecloth or fine sieve, and discard the seeds and fibers. Sometimes lemon juice mixed with a little sugar is substituted for tamarind.

Ganesha, remover of obstacles

SNACKS AND APPETIZERS

FRIED NEPALI CRACKERS
(Nimki)

½ tsp black cumin seeds
1½ tsp salt
2 cups all-purpose flour

2 tbsp oil
⅜ cup water
oil for frying, approximately
1 cup

Dry-roast the cumin seeds in a heavy skillet over low heat until a pleasant aroma emerges. Remove seeds from skillet and allow to cool, then grind to a powder in a coffee mill or mortar.

Blend ground cumin and salt together. Sift and measure flour, and then add cumin and salt to the flour. Heat 2 tablespoons oil and add to the flour, mixing well. Add water little by little to make a dough. Cover for 10 minutes.

Heat 1 cup oil in a skillet. Make small balls of dough and cut with a knife vertically and horizontally, making diamond shapes. When the oil is hot, put 15 to 20 pieces in at a time. When the pieces swell, turn them and when they get slightly brown, remove from the skillet and drain. Follow the same procedure for the remainder of the dough. Serve hot, or store in a tight container.

RICE PANCAKE
(Chatamari)

2 cups rice flour
1 ½ cups water
1 tbsp clarified butter

Mix rice flour and water until they make a smooth batter. Melt some butter in a non-stick frying pan. Pour enough batter to spread into a paper-thin layer (like crepe). Cover with a lid and cook for 2 minutes. This can be served with or without topping. *For variation:* add ½ tablespoon of black lentil flour to the batter.

Topping

½ lb ground meat (pork, lamb, or beef)
½ tsp ground cumin
½ tsp garlic, minced

½ tsp fresh ginger, minced
½ tsp black pepper
salt to taste
1 tbsp oil

Chatamari can be served plain or with a topping of ground meat. To prepare *chatamari* with the topping, add all the above ingredients except the oil to the ground meat, and knead for 10 to 15 minutes, until the color of the meat becomes light. Add the oil and knead for another 2 to 3 minutes. Melt butter in a non-stick pan, and pour in a thin layer of batter as described above. Remove the pan from the heat and use a tablespoon to sprinkle the meat mixture in the batter. Cover tightly and return to low heat. Cook for 3 to 4 minutes. Serve immediately with a pickle relish.

MO MO (STEAMED DUMPLINGS)
(Mo Mo)

Wrappers

2 cups unbleached all-purpose
  flour
3/4 cup water

> **M**ix the flour and water together in a bowl. Knead the
> dough and then form it into a ball. Cover it and let it sit
> for an hour. As an alternative, wonton wrapper skins,
> available in most supermarkets, may be used.

Filling

3/4 cup cabbage, finely chopped
  (optional)
3/4 cup cauliflower, finely
  chopped (optional)
1/2 lb ground turkey
1 medium onion, finely
  shredded
1/2 tbsp black pepper

1/2 tsp turmeric
1 1/2 tsp ground cumin
1/2 tsp cinnamon (optional)
1 tsp curry powder
1/2 cup vegetable oil
1/4 cup water
salt to taste
ground red chili to taste

> **A**dd chopped cabbage and cauliflower to boiling water
> in a sauce pan. Turn down heat and simmer for 3 min-
> utes, then drain completely. Mix all the remaining filling
> ingredients thoroughly in a bowl.
>
> Roll the dough to an even thickness of about 3/16 inch (2
> mm). Cut out 3-inch rounds with a cookie cutter. Put a
> scoop of filling in the center of each piece of dough. Fold
> it in half or in a triangle shape and seal edges. Make sure
> the filling is sealed tight in the dough.

Coat the surface of the steamer rack with vegetable oil so that the Mo Mo will not stick to it when cooked. Place the Mo Mo on the steamer rack so that they do not touch each other. Make sure the water is already boiling before you put the Mo Mo in. Steam for 6 minutes (the time is critical).

TURKEY MO MO
(Turkey Ko Mamacha)

Filling

1 lb ground turkey
$^{1}/_{4}$ cup onion, diced
4 tbsp scallion, diced
1 tbsp ginger root, grated
2 tbsp cilantro, finely chopped
1 tbsp garlic, minced

$^{1}/_{4}$ tsp turmeric
salt to taste
$^{1}/_{4}$ tsp each ground pepper,
    cumin, coriander, and
    cinnamon
2 tbsp vegetable oil

Wrappers

40 wonton skins (approxi-
    mately 3$^{1}/_{2}$ -inch squares)

Mix all filling ingredients very thoroughly. Put 1 teaspoon of turkey mixture in the middle of wrapper. Moisten the inner edges of the wrapper, gather the edges together and pinch the tip to make sure it is sealed. Steam the dumplings over high heat for 15 to 20 minutes. Serve with Tomato and Cilantro Chutney (page 95).

LAMB OR PORK MO MO
(Mamacha)

Wrappers

2¹/₂ cups all-purpose flour
1 tbsp oil (optional)

1 tsp salt
1 cup lukewarm water

Sift flour and salt together in a bowl. Mix with water and oil until the dough is firm but not stiff. Knead for at least 7 minutes. Form dough into a ball. Cover with clear plastic wrap and let it stand for more than 1 hour. Alternatively, wonton wrapper skins may be used.

Filling

1¹/₂ lbs finely minced lamb or pork
4 scallions, including green leaves, finely chopped
1 tbsp fresh ginger, crushed
1¹/₂ tsp garlic, minced
1¹/₂ tsp salt, or to taste
¹/₂ cup fresh cilantro, finely chopped

2 green chilies, seeded and finely chopped
1 tsp *garam masala*
1 tsp ground coriander
1 tsp ground cumin
2 tbsp oil (optional; add only if you want dumplings juicy)
¹/₂ cup water

Combine all ingredients, mixing thoroughly. Cut the dough into small pieces. Roll each piece out as thin as you can on a floured board. Place 1 tablespoon of filling in the center of each wrapper. Gather up the sides into little pleats to cover the filling. Bring water to a boil in a steamer. Place dumplings on the steamer rack and steam for 5 to 7 minutes. Serve with Tomato and Cilantro Chutney (page 95).

FRIED RICE FLAKES
(Tare Ko Chiura)

1¹/₂ **cups rice flakes (***chiura***)**
3 tbsp sugar
oil for deep frying

Heat oil in a heavy saucepan. Pour ¹/₂ cup of rice flakes into the oil, quickly turning it until it becomes white and puffs up. Remove from oil and drain on paper towels. Repeat the process for the remaining quantity. Mix with sugar and serve as a snack. Fried *chiura* can be preserved in an airtight container.

Chiura, *also called flat or beaten rice, is a very common food eaten in Nepal either as a snack or in a full meal with meat, vegetables, eggs, pickle, and so on. It is available at most Indian groceries.*

MIXED VEGETABLE FRITTERS
(Mismas Tarkari Ko Pakoda)

1½ cup chickpea or lentil (*gram*) flour
½ tsp ground cumin
½ tsp ground red chili
1 tsp salt
1 egg
½ cup water

½ cup cauliflower, cut into small pieces
½ cup bell pepper, cut into small pieces
½ cup green onions, chopped
½ cup broccoli, cut into small pieces
1 cup oil for deep frying

Sift flour with cumin, chili, and salt. Mix with the egg and add water little by little, making a light paste. Add all the vegetables and mix thoroughly. Let stand for 15 minutes. Heat oil in a frying pan just to the smoking point. Drop vegetable mixture into the hot oil by the spoonful, cooking no more than 6 to 8 fritters at a time. Fry over medium heat until both sides of the fritters are light brown. Drain on paper towels and serve with chutney.

TURKEY TURNOVERS
(Sya Pali)

Filling

½ lb raw ground turkey
1 medium onion, finely
  shredded
salt and ground red chili to
  taste
¼ teaspoon black pepper

½ teaspoon turmeric
1 teaspoon ground cumin
¼ teaspoon cinnamon
1 teaspoon curry powder
¼ cup vegetable oil

Mix ingredients thoroughly in a bowl.

Dough

2 cups unbleached flour
¾ cup water

Mix flour and water. Knead into a dough that can be rolled. Let stand for half an hour, covered.

To make the turnovers, take about 2½ tablespoons of dough and roll into a ball. Flatten it down, using fingers and palm, to the thickness of ¼ inch, evenly maintaining circular shape about 4 inches in diameter. Place a tablespoon of filling in the center of the dough. Bring the edges to the center, covering the filling and sealing the edges firmly. Now flatten it again, forming the turnover into a round shape about 5 inches in diameter. Don't worry if the filling gets exposed in places.

Place ½ teaspoon cooking oil in a skillet over medium heat. When the oil is hot, put the turnover in and let it cook for 30 seconds. Flip it over and add a little oil again. Keep flipping over two or three times, until golden.

RICE FLAKES WITH NUTS AND LENTILS
(Furundana)

2 cups lentils
1 cup vegetable oil
6 whole dried red chilies
4 tbsp fresh cilantro, chopped
2 cups rice flakes (*chiura*)
2 cups rice crispies
2 cups crisp potato sticks

¼ cup golden raisins
½ cup cashew nuts
½ cup roasted peanuts
½ tsp ground red chili
½ to 1 tsp ground cumin
1½ tsp salt, or to taste

Soak lentils 3 to 4 hours in water. Drain and spread on layers of paper towels for 1 hour to dry. Heat 3 tablespoons of the oil in a deep pan (preferably a wok). Fry the whole chilies until they are dark, then drain on a paper towel. Fry cilantro until crisp, then drain. Add remaining oil to the pan and fry the lentils one-half cup at a time until crisp. Take out with a slotted spoon and spread on paper towel. Add more oil if necessary, and fry *chiura* one-half cup at a time. Mix all the ingredients together and serve.

Furundana can be stored, sealed in an airtight container, for up to 3 months. If you do not have *chiura*, you can substitute rice crispies, which are added without frying.

BLACK LENTIL PATTIES
(Mas Ko Bara Or Phuraula)

1½ cups black lentils
1 tbsp fresh ginger, crushed
⅛ tsp asafetida powder

2 green chilies (optional)
1½ tsp salt, or to taste
2 cups oil for deep frying

Soak lentils in cold water overnight and then rinse to remove the black seed coats. Drain well, put into electric blender, and grind it finely, adding only as much water as is necessary to facilitate blending. Make a thick, smooth paste. Add ginger, asafetida, green chilies, and salt. Blend until it becomes white and light. With wet hands form mixture into flat patties and drop them into hot oil. Turn them with a spoon until they are light golden brown, then drain on paper towel. Serve hot.

POTATO BALLS FILLED WITH MEAT
(Masu Bhareko Alu Chop)

Filling

1 large onion, diced
1 tsp garlic, minced
1 tsp fresh ginger, minced
1 lb any meat, minced

1 green chili pepper, minced
2 tbsp mustard oil
1 tsp ground black pepper
salt to taste

Fry onion, garlic and ginger in a frying pan until light brown. Add rest of the ingredients and meat. Cook for 10 more minutes or until the meat is dry and cooked. Do not add water. Set aside and let it cool.

Casing

6 to 8 large potatoes
salt and pepper to taste
2 large eggs, beaten

1 cup bread crumbs
oil for deep frying

Boil potatoes until soft and cooked. Peel and mash the potatoes until smooth while they are still hot, adding salt and pepper. Take one handful of mashed potatoes into your palm, flatten it into a round shape, and then form a cup. Put one tablespoon of filling into the cup and close it, smoothing it to form an egg-shaped ball. Dip in beaten egg and roll it in bread crumbs. Deep fry in oil over medium heat until golden brown, then drain on paper towel. Serve hot with Tomato and Cilantro Chutney (page 95).

POTATO-FILLED PASTRIES
(Alu Ko Samosa)

Filling

1 onion, chopped
2 tbsp vegetable oil
1 cup potatoes, diced and
    cooked
1/4 tsp salt, or to taste
1 fresh green chili, chopped
1/4 cup fresh cilantro, chopped

1 tsp fresh ginger, minced
1 tsp garlic, minced
1/4 cup green peas
1 tsp *garam masala*
1 tbsp lemon juice
1/4 cup carrots, cooked and
    diced

Saute onion in oil until soft. Add remaining ingredients, mix well and fry slowly for 5 minutes. Set filling aside to cool.

Pastry dough

2 cups all-purpose flour
1/2 tsp salt
cold water

4 tbsp yogurt
4 tbsp clarified butter
oil for deep frying

Sift flour and salt together, and mix with the butter and yogurt. Add enough cold water to make a stiff dough. Knead the dough until smooth. Roll it out very thin and cut it into 3-inch circles. Place a tablespoon of filling on half of each circle. Wet the edges with a little water, fold the dough circle in half and press the edges together to seal.

Deep fry in hot oil (365°F) a few at a time until light brown. Drain on paper towels and serve hot with Tomato and Cilantro Chutney (page 95).

SEMOLINA PIE
(Suzi Ko Pie)

1 cup semolina
2 tbsp oil
water
1 cup yogurt
½ cup cabbage, grated
4 tsp baking powder
1 tsp green chili paste
2 tsp fresh cilantro, chopped
½ cup potato, grated
1 tsp salt

lemon juice, salt, and sugar
(can be adjusted to your
taste)

Spices to cook
2 tbsp oil
1 tsp cumin seeds
1 tsp sesame seeds
½ tsp asafetida powder
2 whole dried red chilies

Mix semolina and oil. Knead well by hand. Add water and yogurt, mixing well. Add remaining ingredients except spices to semolina.

To cook the spices, heat oil in a saucepan. When the oil is hot, add cumin seeds, sesame seeds, asafetida, and chilies, and cook until the seeds pop. Care should be taken not to burn the spices, as this adds a bitter taste to the food. Cook only until light golden brown and you can smell the aroma.

Add the spices to the semolina mixture and pour into a baking dish. Bake at 400°F for 20 minutes. Check with a toothpick in the center of the pie to see if it is done—if the toothpick comes out clean the pie is ready. Serve hot with garlic bread and salad.

POTATO ROLL
(Alu Ko Chop)

1 to 2 garlic cloves
$^1/_2$ inch fresh ginger
$^1/_2$ tsp turmeric
1 tsp ground red chili, or to taste
1 tsp salt, or to taste
$^1/_2$ cup water
2 tbsp vegetable oil

$^1/_2$ tsp anise seed
1 small onion, diced
1 large tomato, chopped
1 lb red potatoes, chopped
1 cup frozen peas
$^1/_2$ bunch fresh cilantro, diced
1 loaf of sliced bread
oil for deep frying

Grind garlic, ginger, turmeric, chili pepper, and salt in a blender with $^1/_2$ cup water to make a paste. Heat cooking oil in a pan and fry anise seed until brown; reduce heat and then add onion, frying until it starts to look brown. Add tomato and cook 2 minutes. Then pour the spice paste into the pan and stir until water is completely gone. Now add potatoes and peas, and cook for about 5 minutes, making sure that all the ingredients are completely mixed. Add cilantro. When cooked, let it stand to cool.

To form the potato rolls, cut the crust from bread slices. Dip each slice in water just long enough to dampen lightly. Squeeze out the excess water by pressing the slice between your palms. Place a spoonfull of filling in the center of the slice, roll, and seal by pressing edges gently. Repeat the process until the filling is used up. Place the rolls on a tray, keeping them covered with a damp towel until ready to fry.

Heat cooking oil in a deep frying pan and fry several potato rolls at a time over medium heat until they are crisp and brown. If you like, serve with cilantro sauce or tomato chutney.

BARBECUED SHREDDED CHICKEN
(Kukhura Ko Chhwelaa)

2 lbs chicken legs or breast or both
1/2 cup onion, chopped
1/4 cup sliced onion rings
1 tsp garlic, minced
2 tsp ginger, minced
1/2 cup fresh cilantro, chopped
1 tbsp lemon juice
1 tsp ground cumin powder

1/2 tsp black pepper
salt, according to taste
hot pepper (optional)— chopped green or crushed red
1 tbsp vegetable oil
1 tsp cumin seeds
1/8 tsp turmeric

Heat barbecue grill and make sure fire has had time to burn down to glowing coals. Place chicken on a rack above the coals and allow to cook until tender, turning pieces until cooked on both sides. Then bone the chicken and cut it into small pieces. Mix all the seasonings except the cumin seeds and turmeric and add to the chopped chicken.

Heat the oil and fry the cumin seeds just until fragrant. Add the turmeric to the fried cumin. Immediately take it off the fire and add to the meat. Mix thoroughly. Serve with rice flakes (*chiura*) or toasted rice.

SOUPS AND LENTILS

GUNDRUK SOUP
(Gundruk Ko Jhol)

Gundruk

**Mustard leaves, radish leaves,
spinach leaves, cabbage, or
cauliflower leaves.**

Gundruk is cured and dried leafy vegetables. To make gundruk, wash the leafy vegetables and crush or pound into shreds. Put them in an earthen jar or container, keep on pressing the crushed leaves and allow to stand for 1 day. The next day press the leaves a little more. Make sure the lid is tight and allow the jar to stand for another 10 days; by this time the contents will have developed an acid smell. Wrap the leaves in a piece of cloth and put in the sun until they dry.

Soup

1 tbsp oil
1/2 tsp cumin seeds
1 dried red chili pepper
1/2 cup *gundruk*
1/2 cup dried or smoked fish
2 cloves garlic, sliced

1 tbsp fresh ginger, chopped
1 tomato, chopped
2 cups water
salt to taste
fresh cilantro, chopped

Heat oil in a saucepan, add cumin seeds and chili pepper and fry until the pepper starts to be light brown. Add the *gundruk* and fish and fry for 1 minute. Add remaining ingredients; cover and simmer for 10 minutes. Sprinkle with cilantro and serve with rice.

MIXED SPROUTED BEAN SOUP
(Quantee)

½ cup soya beans
½ cup chickpeas
½ cup black-eyed peas
½ cup red kidney beans

½ cup mung beans
½ cup whole peas, yellow or green
½ cup lima beans (optional)

Note: For strong taste add more small beans. For mild taste add larger beans.

Mix all the beans together and soak in water in a large container for about 12 hours, or until the beans are soft. Wash thoroughly, drain the water, keep the container covered until the beans sprout. Taste varies with the length of the sprout—¼ inch sprout is the best.

Cooking Method

1 tbsp clarified butter or oil
1 tsp cumin seeds
pinch of lovage seeds (*jwanu*), crushed
1 tsp curry powder
1½ tbsp fresh ginger, minced

3 to 4 cloves garlic, sliced thinly
2 cups sprouted beans
5 cups water
salt to taste

In a heavy skillet heat the oil, fry cumin and lovage just until seeds are light brown. Add the sprouts and cook over medium heat until they are light brown. Add the remaining spices and enough water to cover the bean sprouts. Simmer until the sprouts are soft, adding water as necessary. The finished soup should not be thick, but should have the consistency of vegetable soup. Serve with rice.

SPLIT BLACK LENTILS
(Kalo Maas Ko Dal)

1½ cups black lentils
4 to 5 cups of water (more can be added to dilute, according to taste)
1 tbsp fresh ginger, minced
½ tsp turmeric

6 tbsp clarified butter
salt to taste
¼ tsp asafetida
2 dried red chilies
¼ tsp *jimbu*
1 tsp garlic, minced

Wash lentils thoroughly, removing those that float on the surface, and drain well. Boil water in a saucepan and add drained lentils; bring to a boil again. Add the ginger, turmeric, 3 tablespoons clarified butter, salt, and asafetida. Reduce the heat and simmer, covered, for 20 to 30 minutes until lentils are soft and the consistency is similar to porridge. In a small pan heat the remaining 3 tablespoons of butter and fry the red chilies, *jimbu*, and garlic. Stir into the lentils, mixing well. Serve with rice.

YELLOW LENTILS
(Toor Dal)

4 cups water
1 cup yellow lentils (*toor dal*)
1 tbsp butter
¹/₂ tsp salt
¹/₄ tsp tumeric
¹/₄ onion, chopped
1 or 2 tomatoes, diced
   (optional)

2 cloves
¹/₂ tsp cumin seeds
1 stick cinnamon
2 cardamon pods
1 tbsp butter

Warm water in a saucepan and add lentils, butter, salt, and tumeric. Cover and simmer over low heat for 40 minutes to one hour. In a small heavy pan, fry onion in 1 tablespoon butter until brown. Add cloves, cumin, cinnamon, and cardamon and fry for a few seconds. Add tomato (if desired). Stir this spice mixture into the cooked lentils, cover, and allow the seasonings to flavor the lentils. Stir and serve with rice or chapati.

This is a basic recipe that also works well with urad, moong, *and* mussoor dal. *For an alternate method in which the* dal *cooks together with the spices, see Mixed Dal, page 36.*

MIXED DAL
(Mismas Dal)

2 tbsp clarified butter
1 stick cinnamon
2 bay leaves
½ tsp cumin seeds
2 cardamom pods, crushed
1 medium onion, finely
   minced
1 tbsp fresh ginger, finely
   grated
½ tsp turmeric
salt to taste

⅛ tsp asafetida
2 tomatoes, chopped
2 tbsp *urad dal*
2 tbsp *mussoor dal*
2 tbsp *toor dal*
2 tbsp *moong dal*
2 tbsp *chana dal*
5 cups hot water
1 tbsp lemon juice or tamarind
   pulp

Heat clarified butter in a saucepan and fry the cinnamon stick, bay leaves, cumin seeds, and cardamom. Add the onion and ginger, and fry until golden brown. Add the turmeric, salt, asafetida, and tomato, and cook until the tomato is soft. Add washed and drained lentils, frying them for 2 minutes. Pour in hot water, bring it to a boil, then reduce heat and simmer for 20 minutes or until the lentils are cooked. Add the lemon juice and serve with rice.

Lentils, beans, and chickpeas, or dal in Nepali, are available in many varieties from Indian groceries and many supermarkets. Each has a distinctive taste and texture. Urad dal *refers to split black lentils with the skins removed;* mussoor dal *to orange lentils;* toor dal *to yellow lentils;* moong dal, *also called mung beans, are split, with the skins removed;* chana dal *are small chickpeas, split, with the skins removed.*

SUN-DRIED LENTIL AND VEGETABLE BALLS WITH POTATO
(Maseura Ra Alu Ko Takari)

1 cup sun-dried lentil and
  vegetable balls (see page 38)
2 tbsp vegetable oil
$1/8$ tsp lovage seeds (*jwano*)
2 medium potatoes, cut into
  1-inch cubes
1 medium tomato, chopped
1 $1/4$ tsp ground red chili, or to
  taste

$1/2$ tsp ground cumin
$1/2$ tsp ground coriander
$1/8$ tsp turmeric
1 inch fresh ginger, finely
  diced
2 cloves garlic, finely diced
2 cups water
1 tbsp fresh cilantro, chopped

Heat 1 tablespoon of oil in a heavy skillet over medium heat. Fry the lentil and vegetable balls until golden brown. Remove from the pan and set aside.

Add remaining 1 tablespoon oil to the skillet. Fry lovage seeds for 10 seconds. Add potatoes and cook until light brown. Add tomato, and cook, covered, for 3 minutes. Add all spices, including ginger and garlic, cover, and cook for 2 more minutes. Then add fried lentil balls and water. Cover and cook 10 minutes. Add cilantro at the end. Serve with rice or chapati (page 121).

SUN-DRIED LENTIL AND VEGETABLE BALLS
(Maseura)

4 cups black lentils (*mas dal*)
2 cups finely chopped vegetables (choose any from
  leek, scallion, spinach,
  onion, or cauliflower

Soak the lentils overnight. Wash and remove the skins. Grind in a blender, using as little water as possible, to make a thick paste. Finely chop the vegetables and mix with lentil paste. Form into small balls (1 inch in diameter) and place on a microwaveable flat dish. Microwave for 2-3 minutes, then leave to dry in a sunny area or place in a food dehydrator. (Food dehydrator works best for drying.) When completely dry, store in an airtight container. Dried lentil and vegetable balls will keep for up to six months.

SPICY SPINACH LENTILS
(Dal Ra Palungo)

ed butter or oil
. cinnamon
s
n seeds

n pods
onion, chopped
h ginger, chopped

1/3 tsp turmeric
2 tsp salt, or to taste
8 oz spinach, chopped
2 cups yellow lentils (*toor dal*; yellow split peas can be substituted)
4 cups water

sh lentils and drain well. Boil 4 cups of water in a
epan. Add drained lentils and bring to a boil. Add
of the turmeric and half of the salt. Cook covered for
an hour, adding more water if needed.

hile lentils are cooking, heat clarified butter just to
king, reduce heat to medium, and fry cinnamon, bay
es, cumin seeds, cloves and cardamom. Add onion
ginger. Cook until golden brown. Add half of the
eric, half of the salt, and the spinach. Cook until spin-
is soft and set aside.

hen lentils are almost done, add the reserved spin-
and cook for 5 more minutes. Serve warm with rice
hapati. Can also be served as soup.

MUNG BEAN BALLS
(Titura)

4 cups split mung beans or green lentils (*moong dal*)
1 tsp cumin seed

1/8 tsp asafetida
1/4 tsp ground red chili (optional)

Soak lentils overnight. Wash and remove skins and grind in a blender to make a smooth paste. Add cumin, asafetida and chili and blend well. Form into balls the size of a small marble and place on a greased microwaveable dish. Microwave 2-3 minutes and dry in a sunny area or food dehydrator. Store in an airtight container. Can be cooked in the same way as dried lentil and vegetable balls (see recipe on page 37).

GROUND TURKEY WITH MIXED BEAN SOUP

(Keema Quantee)

¼ cup whole mung beans

¼ cup whole black lentils

¼ cup whole soya beans

¼ cup whole black-eyed peas

¼ cup whole cow peas

¼ cup field pea (small variety of peas)

¼ cup fava beans

¼ cup whole red kidney beans

Soak the beans in water for 24 hours until they swell to double the size. Wash thoroughly and drain water. Wrap the beans in muslin cloth and place in a warm place to sprout (about 2 days).

2 tbsp oil

¼ tsp cumin seeds

¼ tsp lovage seeds

2 cups of mixed sprouted beans (save the rest for later)

2 cloves garlic, ground

2 tbsp fresh ginger, ground

2 tsp ground cumin

4 cups water

2 tsp ground coriander

salt to taste

½ tsp turmeric

⅓ lb ground, lean turkey or chicken

cilantro, chopped (to garnish)

In a heavy skillet or pressure cooker heat 1 tablespoon of oil and fry cumin and lovage seeds until golden brown. Add sprouted beans and fry for 4 minutes. Add remaining ingredients except meat and cilantro. If using a pressure cooker, cook for 10 minutes; in a heavy skillet, cook until beans are soft.

Meanwhile, heat 1 tablespoon oil an
in a separate saucepan until brown. Ac
and cook for another 5 minutes. Gar
Serve with rice.

FRIED LENTIL F
WITH YOGU
(Kadi Badi Ko J

1 cup black lentils (*urad dal*)

salt to taste

¾ tsp ground cumin

¼ tsp ground coriander

ground red chili (optional)

oil for deep frying

2 cups yogurt

4 cups

1 tsp

1 tsp

½ tsp

3 wh

¼ tsp

Soak lentils for 5 hours or more. Dr
blend the lentils to a paste, adding
sible. Add salt, cumin, coriander, a
well. Deep fry small balls (½ inch in
in medium heat until golden brown

Mix yogurt with 4 cups of water i
consistency. In a saucepan, heat
fenugreek, cumin seed, whole red c
beaten yogurt mixture to oil (cove
adding yogurt to avoid oil splash
Add lentil balls. Serve with rice, o

2 tsp

1 inch

2 bay

½ tsp

3 clove

2 card

1 medi

½ inch

s

h

h

sɪ

le

aɪ

tu

ac

ac

or

VEGETABLES

MIXED VEGETABLE CURRY
(Mismas Tarkari)

1 cup cabbage, chopped
1 cup green beans
l cup cauliflower, chopped
1 cup green peas
2 medium potatoes, peeled and diced into cubes
3 tbsp vegetable oil (preferably corn oil)
2 medium onions, thinly sliced
1 tsp green pepper, chopped
1 tbsp ground coriander
$1/2$ tbsp ground cumin
$1/4$ tsp ground cinnamon
$1/4$ tsp ground cardamom
$1/8$ tsp ground cloves
$1/2$ tsp ground red chili
$1/2$ tsp fesh ginger, finely chopped
salt to taste
$1^1/2$ cup thick coconut milk
juice of $1/2$ lemon
2 tbsp cilantro, finely chopped

Combine the cabbage, beans, cauliflower, peas, and potatoes. Add just enough water to cook without burning and simmer for 5 minutes. Drain.

In another pot, heat the oil and fry the vegetables until golden brown. Add green pepper, spices, cooked vegetables, and salt. Fry for several minutes, stirring frequently, and then put in coconut milk. Simmer gently until vegetables are tender, watching carefully to prevent burning. Remove from heat and add lemon juice. Garnish with cilantro.

HOT POTATO CURRY
(Aloo Ko Piro Tarkari)

1 lb potatoes
2 tbsp oil
3 cloves garlic, diced
1 tbsp fresh ginger, crushed

salt to taste
$\frac{1}{2}$ tsp turmeric powder
4 to 5 green chili peppers
$\frac{1}{2}$ cup fresh cilantro, chopped

Cut potatoes lengthwise into 4 to 5 pieces. Heat the oil in a heavy skillet. Add potatoes and remaining ingredients. Cover and cook over low heat until potatoes are cooked (20-25 minutes). Garnish with cilantro and serve.

STUFFED BITTER MELON
(Bhareko Karela)

4 bitter melons
1 tbsp salt

Slit bitter melons lengthwise. Remove seeds and pulp. Sprinkle with salt and let it stand overnight. Drain the excess water out.

Stuffing

2 medium potatoes, boiled and mashed
1 onion, chopped
1/2 cup green peas

1/2 tsp each ground red chili, fresh garlic, and fresh ginger
salt to taste

Mix the above ingredients, stuff inside the bitter melon and tie the halves of each melon together with string. Deep fry over medium heat until brown. Serve warm.

Bitter melons, also called bitter gourds, bitter cucumbers, and balsam pears, resemble cucumbers with bumpy skins. They are available in Indian and Chinese grocery stores. To lessen the bitterness of this vegetable, it is often boiled in salted water before cooking.

CREAMY ONIONS
(Makkhani Pyaz)

16 small white onions
2¹/₂ cups light chicken stock
6 cloves

Place the onions in a saucepan with the chicken stock and cloves. Bring the stock to a boil, then reduce the heat and simmer until the onions are just tender. Drain the onions, strain and reserve the stock.

Sauce

1 tbsp butter
1 tbsp flour
2 tbsp milk
onion/chicken stock (*see instructions above*)

1¹/₄ cups cream
sherry to taste
freshly ground pepper

Melt the butter in a small pan and stir in flour. Cook a little, then whisk in the milk, reserved stock, cream, sherry, and pepper to taste. Stir well, bring to a boil, and cook for a few minutes. Pour over the onions. Serve hot as a vegetable or cold as a salad.

MUSHROOM AND POTATO CURRY
(Chyau Alu Ko Tarkari)

5 medium potatoes
2 tbsp oil
$^1/_4$ tsp fenugreek seeds
$^1/_8$ tsp szechwan pepper
4 green chili peppers, sliced
1 tbsp ground cumin

$^1/_4$ tsp turmeric
salt to taste
4 medium onions, chopped
1 lb mushrooms
2 ripe tomatoes, chopped
2 whole dried red chilies

Peel potatoes and cut into quarters. In a heavy saucepan with lid, heat oil and fry fenugreek seeds and szechwan pepper until golden brown. Add green chili slices, potatoes, cumin, turmeric, and salt. Simmer for 5 minutes. Add onions, mushrooms, tomatoes, and red chilies. Cover and cook until done.

SCALLOPED POTATOES WITH CHEESE AND HERBS
(Masala Panir Alu)

3 tbsp butter
2 onions, finely chopped
2 cloves garlic, minced
3 cups milk
$1/4$ tsp dried rosemary
$1/4$ tsp dried basil

$1/4$ tsp dried oregano
1 tsp salt
$1/4$ tsp black pepper
2 cups grated Swiss cheese
1 cup fresh bread crumbs
5 medium potatoes

Melt butter in skillet and cook the onions and garlic until tender without browning. Heat the milk, rosemary, basil, oregano, salt, and pepper in a saucepan. In a separate dish, combine the cheese and bread crumbs.

Peel potatoes and slice thinly. Place one-third of potatoes in bottom of a buttered casserole, spread half the onions over potatoes and sprinkle with a third of the cheese mixture. Place another third of potatoes on top; the remaining onions on top of that, and another third of the cheese. Add the remaining potatoes, and pour milk mixture over them; sprinkle with remaining cheese. Bake at 350°F for 1 hour and 35 minutes or until potatoes are tender when pierced with a knife. Let the dish sit 10 minutes before serving.

CHICKPEA CURRY
(Kabuli Chana Ko Tarkari)

1 cup dried brown chickpeas,
  soaked overnight
3 to 4 cups water
2 tbsp oil
2 medium onions, finely
  chopped
2 tsp garlic, diced
2 tsp fresh ginger, minced
1 tsp turmeric

1 tsp *garam masala*
1 tsp ground cumin
1 tsp ground coriander
2 tsp salt, or to taste
3 fresh green chilies (optional)
3 medium ripe tomatoes,
  chopped
juice of 1 lemon
$^1/_2$ cup cilantro, chopped

Cook soaked chickpeas in water until tender. Heat oil in a heavy saucepan and fry the onions, garlic, and ginger until golden brown. Add chopped tomatoes and remaining spices and cook for a few minutes. Add chickpeas together with cooking liquid. Cover and simmer on low heat for another 10 to 15 minutes. Add lemon juice and cilantro.

PAN-FRIED ASPARAGUS AND POTATOES
(Kurilo Alu Bhutuwa)

2 tbsp corn oil
$^1/_8$ tsp black cumin seeds
$^1/_8$ tsp cumin seeds
2 medium potatoes, cut into
   long pieces
2 lbs asparagus, cut into thin
   long pieces (quartered)

1 tsp ground red chili
$^1/_4$ tsp turmeric
salt to taste
$^1/_2$ tsp ground cumin
$^1/_2$ tsp ground coriander
$^1/_2$ inch fresh ginger, crushed
2 small cloves garlic, crushed

In a large saucepan (preferably non-stick), heat oil and fry black cumin and cumin for a few seconds. Add potatoes and fry until light brown. Add asparagus and cook, covered, over medium heat for 2 minutes. Add chili powder, turmeric, and salt. Cook covered 2 more minutes and add ground cumin and coriander. Cook covered for about 8 minutes, or until asparagus is soft. Add crushed ginger and garlic, and stirring frequently, cook until the asparagus turns brownish (not burned).

POTATO KABAB
(Alu Kabab)

6 medium potatoes
1 tbsp cumin powder
1 tbsp ground coriander
$^1/_2$ inch fresh ginger, crushed
5 cloves garlic, crushed
1 cup yogurt
$^1/_4$ tsp ground black pepper

ground red pepper to taste
$^1/_4$ tsp turmeric
salt to taste
4 small bay leaves
$^1/_2$ cup oil
$^1/_2$ inch fresh ginger, chopped

Peel potatoes and cut each potato into 4 equal pieces. In a large bowl, mix cumin, coriander, crushed ginger, garlic, yogurt, black pepper, red pepper, turmeric and salt. Add the potatoes, mix thoroughly, and allow them to marinate for 4 hours.

In a large saucepan, heat oil, add chopped ginger and let it brown over high heat. Add the bay leaves and cook briefly. Add the potato mixture and cook until the potatoes are light golden brown, stirring occasionally. Cover pan tightly and turn heat to low for 10 to 15 minutes. The potatoes should be dry, tender, and golden brown. Serve hot with rice or rice flakes.

POTATO, TOMATO AND ONION CURRY
(Alu Golbheda Ra Pyaj Ko Tarkari)

3 tbsp oil or clarified butter
3 medium onions, cut in large
  pieces
1 lb medium potatoes, cut in
  large pieces
2 tsp salt
$^1/_2$ tsp ground red pepper
$^1/_2$ tsp turmeric

1 lb tomatoes, cut in wedges
3 green chili peppers, finely
  sliced
1 tbsp fresh ginger, finely
  chopped
1 tsp sugar
$^1/_2$ tsp *garam masala*
$^1/_4$ cup fresh cilantro, chopped

Heat oil or butter in a heavy pan. Add onions and cook over high heat. Add potatoes, salt, red pepper, and turmeric. Reduce heat to medium and cover pan. Do not add any water. When the potatoes are nearly cooked, add tomatoes, green chilies, ginger, and sugar. Turn heat to high and continue cooking uncovered. The potatoes, though cooked, should remain firm. Serve sprinkled with *garam masala* and cilantro.

ELEPHANT-EAR LEAVES AND STEM CURRY
(Karkalo Ra Gaba Ko Tarkari)

3 to 4 whole, fresh young
  karkalo leaves
3 cups fresh young *karkalo*
  stems, chopped
2 cups water
1 tsp fresh ginger, finely
  grated
salt to taste

2 tbsp mustard oil
1 dried red chili pepper
$\frac{1}{4}$ tsp fenugreek seeds
$\frac{1}{4}$ tsp lovage seeds (*jwanu*)
$\frac{1}{4}$ tsp *jimbu*
$\frac{1}{8}$ tsp asafetida
juice of 1 lemon

Wash, cut, and peel off outer covering of the *karkalo* stems. Roll the young *karkalo* leaves and tie the two ends into a knot. Drop both into boiling water in a saucepan, and cook until the leaves become like a paste. Add ginger and salt.

In another pan, heat oil and fry the seeds, chili, and spices until light golden brown. Add to *karkalo* paste. Add lemon juice and mix well. Serve with rice.

Karkalo *is the Nepali name for elephant-ear leaves, taro leaves, or* arbi patla *as they are called in Indian groceries. They are green, heart-shaped leaves 15 to 18 inches long.*

SUN-DRIED POTATO CURRY
(Alu Golbheda Ra Pyaj Ko Tarkari)

1 lb potatoes

Wash and boil potatoes. Potatoes should be mature and heavy for their size and free from bruises or decay. If potatoes are not boiled enough, they will turn black during drying and storage. Peel and slice, or grate and make tiny balls, and sun dry the potatoes in sunny place until dry and crisp. Store in an airtight container.

2 tbsp clarified butter
1/8 tsp fenugreek seeds
1 dried red chili (optional)
2 cups sun-dried potatoes
1 tsp fresh ginger, crushed

1/2 tsp ground cumin
salt to taste
1 tomato, finely chopped
1 1/2 cups water
1/2 cup fresh cilantro, chopped

Heat clarified butter over a medium flame. Fry fenugreek seeds and red chili until the color changes. Add dried potato and fry for 1 minute. Add ginger, cumin, and salt, frying them for 1/2 minute. Add tomato and water to make a soup. Garnish with cilantro. Serve with rice.

PUMPKIN VINE TIPS
(Pharsi Munta Ko Tarkari)

3 cups pumpkin vine tips
2 tbsp clarified butter
$^1/_2$ tsp fenugreek seeds
1 dried red chili pepper
1 tsp fresh ginger, finely
   crushed

1 tsp ground cumin
$^1/_8$ tsp turmeric
salt to taste

Cut and peel outer covering of the vine stems and break into small pieces along with tender leaves. Heat clarified butter in a heavy saucepan and add fenugreek seeds and chili, cooking until they become dark golden brown. Add vine tips, ginger, cumin, turmeric, and salt. Cover the saucepan and cook just until everything becomes tender. Do not overcook. Can be served as a side dish with rice.

Pumpkin vine tips are harvested from the growing end of the pumpkin vine. Several vines are required. Pinch the tender end (up to 1 foot) off the vine. Both the tender leaves and stems are eaten. The pumpkin vine will put out new shoots after the tips are harvested.

CAULIFLOWER AND POTATO CURRY
(Alu Kauli Ko Tarkari)

1 medium-size cauliflower
2 potatoes
2 tbsp vegetable oil
$\frac{1}{4}$ tsp cumin seeds
1 bay leaf
$\frac{1}{2}$ tsp turmeric
$\frac{3}{4}$ tsp salt, or to taste
$\frac{1}{2}$ tsp fresh ginger, crushed

3 cloves garlic, crushed
2 green chilies or $\frac{1}{2}$ tsp ground red chili
$\frac{1}{2}$ cup green peas, fresh or frozen
1 tsp *garam masala*
cilantro

Cut cauliflower into florets. Peel and cut potatoes lengthwise. Heat oil in a pan and fry cumin seeds and bay leaf. Add potatoes and fry for 2 minutes. Add cauliflower, turmeric, and salt; cover and cook for 5 minutes. Add ginger, garlic, green or red pepper, green peas, and *garam masala*. Cover and cook for 10 minutes. Garnish with chopped cilantro. Serve with rice or chapati (page 121).

MUSTARD GREENS
(Rayo Ko Saag)

4 cups washed and coarsely
  cut mustard greens
1½ tbsp oil (mustard oil
  preferred)
1 dried red chili pepper
1 tsp cumin seeds

½ tsp lovage seeds
1 tsp ground cumin
1 tsp ground ginger
salt to taste
⅛ tsp turmeric

Wash the mustard greens and drain. Heat oil in a heavy saucepan and fry red chili, cumin seeds, and lovage seeds until they become golden brown. Add mustard greens and stir well. Add the remaining spices, cover tightly, and cook for 5 minutes. Serve hot with rice.

PAN-FRIED OKRA
(Tare Ko Ramtoriya)

2 cups fresh okra *or* 1 lb frozen
4 tbsp mustard or corn oil
   (more oil required for
   frozen okra)
¹/₂ tsp cumin seeds
¹/₂ tsp lovage seeds

1 tsp fresh ginger, crushed
¹/₂ tsp turmeric
¹/₂ tsp ground cumin
salt to taste
¹/₂ tsp ground red chili

Wash fresh okra before cutting into small pieces. Heat oil and fry cumin and lovage seeds until golden brown. Add okra and fry over medium heat until brown and tender. Add all the remaining ingredients and cook for a few more minutes.

BAMBOO-SHOOT MEDLEY
(Tama Ko Tarkari)

2¹/₂ tbsp mustard or corn oil
1 medium onion, finely sliced
1 tbsp fresh ginger, minced
1 tbsp ground cumin
¹/₂ tsp turmeric
¹/₂ tsp ground coriander
¹/₂ tsp ground red chili
salt to taste
2 medium-size potatoes, cut
  into round pieces

1 cup black-eyed peas, soaked
  overnight
1 ripe tomato
1¹/₂ cups water
¹/₂ cup bamboo shoots (canned
  or preserved; can be bought
  in any Asian grocery)

Fry onion in a heavy saucepan until it is golden brown.
Add ginger, cumin, turmeric, coriander, chili, and salt.
Fry briefly over medium heat. Add potatoes, beans, and
tomato, and cook until tender. Add water, and when it
starts boiling, add bamboo shoots. Cover and cook for a
few minutes. Serve with rice.

SPICY WHOLE POTATOES
(Alu Dum)

1 lb small new potatoes
3 tbsp oil
1½ inches cinnamon stick
2 green cardamom pods
4 whole cloves
1 bay leaf
1 can (8 oz) whole tomatoes or
    4 fresh tomatoes, chopped

2 green peppers, chopped
1 tsp fresh ginger, chopped
1 tsp garlic, chopped
2 cups onions, chopped
1 tbsp *garam masala*
½ tsp turmeric
salt to taste

Boil potatoes with skin in just enough water to almost cover them; when cooked, drain and skin potatoes. Fry potatoes in 2 tablespoons oil over medium heat until golden brown. Heat 1 tablespoon oil in another saucepan and fry the cinnamon, cardamom, cloves and bay leaf for 1 minute. Add tomatoes and remaining ingredients. Cover and cook over medium heat for 15 to 20 minutes, or until potatoes are cooked.

PEAS AND TOFU CURRY
(Kerau Ra Tofu Tarkari)

oil for frying
2 cups tofu (bean curd), cut
   into cubes
1 inch fresh ginger
2 cloves garlic
1/2 tsp turmeric
1 tsp ground cumin
2 onions, finely chopped
2 cardamom pods

2 bay leaves
1 tsp salt, or to taste
chopped cilantro
2 cups peas
4 tomatoes, chopped
2 cups water
1/2 tsp each ground red chili
   and ground coriander
1 tsp *garam masala*

Heat oil and fry tofu cubes until golden; remove from pan and drain. Grind ginger, garlic, turmeric, and cumin to make a paste. Reheat oil and fry onion, cardamom, and bay leaves until onions are golden; then add the paste and salt, and fry for another minute. Add peas and tomatoes, and cook for 2 minutes. Add water, cover, and cook until peas are tender. Add tofu cubes and remaining spices, cover, and cook for 2 more minutes. Garnish with cilantro. Serve with bread or rice.

CHICKPEA CURRY
(Thulo Chana Ko Tarkari)

¼ cup vegetable oil
¼ tsp lovage seeds
1 tsp garlic, finely chopped
2 tsp fresh ginger, finely
  minced
3 medium onions, finely sliced
  (reserve 2 tbsp for garnish)
¼ tsp turmeric
salt to taste
2 tsp each ground cumin,
  coriander, pepper

¼ tsp each ground cloves,
  cardamom, cumin, mace
2 cups chickpeas, soaked
  overnight
2 tbsp tomato paste
2 tbsp plain yogurt
2 tsp chopped cilantro
2 tbsp lemon juice
2 green chilies, finely chopped
2 tbsp sliced onions, to garnish
1 cup water

Heat oil in an uncovered 6-quart pressure cooker and fry lovage seeds until light brown. Add garlic, ginger, and onions, and fry until onion is soft. Add turmeric, salt, spices, chickpeas, and water. Place lid on pressure cooker, and pressure-cook over medium heat for 8 to 10 minutes. (If canned chickpeas are used, pressure cooking is not necessary.) After the chickpeas are soft, add tomato paste and yogurt, and cook for another 6 to 8 minutes. Remove the cover and continue cooking over low heat for another 10 minutes, adding water if necessary. Remove from heat and add cilantro and lemon juice. Garish with green chilies and sliced onions.

TOFU, CAULIFLOWER, AND MUSHROOM STIR-FRY
(Tofu Kauli Ra Chyau Ko Tarkari)

2 tbsp olive oil
1 cup firm tofu, diced
1 onion, diced
$^2/_3$ cup cauliflower, chopped
1 tsp ground ginger
$^1/_2$ tsp ground black pepper

1 tsp garlic, diced
$^2/_3$ cup mushrooms, chopped
1 large tomato, chopped
1 green pepper, chopped
$^1/_2$ cup fresh or frozen peas

Heat oil in a heavy skillet over medium heat. Add tofu, and remove when tofu is crisp. Sauté onion until golden, then add cauliflower and spices, and cook 2 minutes. Add mushroom, tomato and green pepper. Cover and cook until vegetables are tender. When nearly done add peas. Serve as a side dish.

MUSTARD GREENS WITH RICE FLOUR SAUCE
(Rayo Sag Ko Bhattal)

1 lb mustard greens
1 tbsp cooking oil
2 dried red chilies
3/4 tsp szechwan pepper,
  ground

2 tbsp rice flour
1/2 tsp salt, or to taste
1 cup water

Wash mustard greens well and cut in small pieces. Heat oil in a saucepan and when hot add chilies and szechwan pepper. Add mustard leaves and cook for 5 minutes over high heat. Mix the rice flour in a bowl with 1 cup of water and pour over the greens. Cook for 10 minutes more over medium heat. Serve hot over rice.

POTATOES AND OKRA WITH SOYBEANS
(Bhatamas Alu Ramtoria Tarkari)

2 tbsp oil
2 medium potatoes, peeled
and cut into ³/₄-inch cubes
¹/₂ lb okra, cut into 1-inch
pieces

1 cup fresh or frozen soybeans
¹/₂ tsp ground cumin
¹/₂ tsp ground coriander
salt to taste

In a saucepan, heat oil. Fry potatoes until light golden in color. Add okra and soybeans. Cook for about 15 minutes over medium heat. Add spices and cook for another 5 minutes or until everything is tender. Serve with rice and dal.

PLANTAIN CURRY
(Kera Ko Tarkari)

1/2 cup dry chickpeas (*chana dal*)
1 tsp cumin seeds
1 inch fresh ginger, crushed
2 plantains
2 small potatoes
1/2 tsp turmeric
3 green chilies, cut lengthwise

2 bay leaves
1/2 tsp *garam masala*
3 tbsp oil
1 tbsp clarified butter
salt and ground red chili to taste
1 tbsp cilantro leaves

Soak chickpeas overnight and boil until soft. Drain, reserving liquid, and set aside.

Grind cumin seeds and ginger to a paste.

Peel and slice plantains and potatoes.

Heat oil in heavy skillet over medium heat and add bay leaves. When they turn brown, add plantains and potatoes. Cook until golden brown. Add all the spices, salt, ginger paste, and tomato. Cook until dry. Cover with 1 cup reserved liquid and cook until the vegetables are almost done. Add the boiled chickpeas and cook, covered, for 5 more minutes. Remove from heat and mix in clarified butter. Serve warm, decorated with cilantro leaves.

GRAPEFRUIT SALAD
(Bhogate Sadeko)

3 tbsp ground sesame seeds
2 cups plain yogurt
½ tsp salt
3 tbsp sugar

2 medium grapefruits, peeled
and cut into small pieces
4 oranges, peeled and cut into
small pieces

Lightly roast sesame seeds and grind to a powder in a coffee mill. Mix sesame seed powder with yogurt, salt and sugar in a bowl. Stir in grapefruit and orange pieces. Chill and serve. For a spicy taste, add some ground red chili. For a different taste, add grapes, sliced in two. Enjoy!

MEAT, CHICKEN, AND SEAFOOD

CHICKEN CURRY
(Kukhura Ko Tarkari)

3 lbs chicken, use a combination of legs, thighs, and breasts
2 tbsp corn oil
1 inch stick cinnamon
3 cardamom pods, bruised
4 cloves
3 medium onions, chopped
salt to taste
1/3 tsp turmeric

1/2 tsp ground red chili
3/4 tsp ground cumin
3/4 tsp ground coriander
2 medium tomatoes, chopped
1 inch fresh ginger, finely grated
4 small cloves garlic, finely grated
1 tbsp fresh cilantro, chopped

Skin and bone the chicken and remove as much fat as possible. Cut into 8 to 10 pieces.

Heat oil over medium heat, and add stick cinnamon, cardamom and cloves. Fry for a few seconds, being careful not to burn. Add chopped onions and fry, stirring until golden brown. Add chicken pieces, turn the heat high, and fry until light brown. Add salt, turmeric, and chili. Turn heat to medium and cook, covered, for about 2 minutes. Add cumin and coriander; cook for 2 minutes and then add chopped tomatoes. Cook covered for 15 minutes. Add ginger and garlic, and cook 10 more minutes. If cooked over medium to medium-low heat, no water is needed. Remove saucepan from heat, and add cilantro. Serve with rice.

SPICY FRIED PORK CUBES
(Bangur Bhutuwa)

2 to 3 lbs pork
$^1/_2$ cup vegetable oil
1 tbsp salt, or to taste
$^1/_4$ tsp turmeric
2 cups water
1 large yellow onion, sliced
$^1/_2$ cup green peas

1 tbsp ground cumin
$^1/_2$ tbsp ground coriander
$1^1/_2$ inches fresh ginger
5 cloves garlic
$^1/_3$ tsp each ground cloves,
    cinnamon, and cardamom

Dice pork into $^1/_2$-inch cubes. Wash well and fry in $^1/_2$ cup oil for 30 seconds, stirring constantly. Add salt, turmeric, and then water. Cover pan and let simmer over medium heat for 10 minutes. Lift cover and cook over high heat until water evaporates, then lower heat to medium and cook pork until it is brown. (Remove excess oil from pan, leaving only about 2 teaspoons.) Add onions and peas while stirring regularly. Add cumin and coriander; then add ginger, garlic and a mixture of the cloves, cinnamon, and cardamom. Cook for 1 more minute.

ROASTED OR GRILLED MEAT
(Sekuwa Masu)

2 to 3 lbs meat (chicken, pork, beef, lamb, or goat)
2 cups yogurt (for chicken; optional for other meat)
1/2 tsp ground cumin
1/2 tsp freshly ground black pepper
1/4 tsp freshly grated nutmeg
1/4 tsp ground cloves
1/2 tsp ground coriander

1 tsp grated fresh ginger, or 1/2 tsp dried
1 clove garlic, finely minced
1/2 tsp cayenne pepper (optional)
salt to taste
1/2 tsp ground cardamom
1/2 cup onion, finely chopped
2 tbsp oil

Remove bones, skin, and fat from the meat. Combine the remaining ingredients and then process to a fine liquid in a blender. Pour the mixture over the meat, turning until it is completely coated. Cover and refrigerate for 24 hours.

Preheat oven to 475°F. Place meat on a baking sheet lined with heavy-duty aluminum foil and bake 25 minutes. If you are using a grill, place it on the grill to cook; then turn it until the meat is thoroughly cooked.

EGG CURRY
(Phul Ko Tarkari)

1½ tbsp oil
1 tbsp butter or clarified butter
1 medium onion, finely
  chopped
2 cloves garlic, crushed
1 inch fresh ginger,
  crushed
½ tsp ground cumin

¼ tsp ground coriander
⅛ tsp turmeric
½ tsp salt
ground red chili to taste
¼ tsp *garam masala*
6 large eggs, beaten
¾ cup green peas, crushed

Heat oil in a heavy frying pan and fry the onion until it is dark golden brown. Add garlic and ginger and fry 2 more minutes. Mix in the remaining ingredients except the peas and eggs, and fry 1 more minute. Slowly pour in the beaten eggs, mixing them well with the onion and spices. Cook another 15 minutes, stirring frequently. Add the crushed peas, and cook 10 minutes over low heat. When ready, the curry should taste like fish rather than scrambled omelet. Serve hot.

PORK CHOPS AND RICE
(Bangor Ko Masu Bhat)

6 medium-size pork chops
$^1/_2$ cup flour
salt and pepper to taste
3 tbsp vegetable oil
2 large onions, finely sliced
2 cloves garlic, crushed
whole dried red chili peppers
$^1/_2$ to 1 tsp paprika
1 tsp oregano

$^1/_2$ tsp thyme
32 oz canned tomatoes
2 cups rice, washed and
    drained
1 cup beef bouillon (or canned
    beef or chicken broth)
1 cup water

Dip pork chops in flour, salt, and pepper, covering well. Brown chops on both sides in a heavy skillet with oil. Remove chops, add onions, garlic, and chilies. Cook until onions are lightly browned. Add paprika, oregano, thyme, and tomatoes and cook 2 more minutes. Add rice, and then the bouillon or broth and water. Bring to a boil and remove from heat. Put the pork chops back in, burying them completely in the rice. Cover skillet with aluminum foil and bake in oven at 350°F for 30 minutes. Vegetables such as peas or green pepper can be added before baking.

LAMB CURRY WITH CAULIFLOWER AND PEAS

(Kauli Matar Ra Masu)

$\frac{1}{2}$ cup oil
1 stick cinnamon
4 whole cloves
2 bay leaves
4 cardamom pods, bruised
1 lb lamb (cut meat into cubes and reserve any bones to cook with meat, as this gives the dish good flavor)
1 tbsp fresh ginger, finely sliced
salt to taste
1 tsp turmeric

1 small cauliflower
1 tbsp fresh ginger, minced
1 tbsp garlic, minced
$\frac{1}{4}$ tsp ground black pepper
1 cup peas (fresh if possible)
1 tbsp ground coriander
1 tbsp ground cumin
1 tsp *garam masala*
2 red chilies (according to taste)
3 to 4 tbsp fresh cilantro, chopped

Heat the oil in a large saucepan and fry the cinnamon, cloves, bay leaves, and cardamom. Continue stirring until golden brown. Add lamb, sliced ginger, salt, and turmeric. Cover and cook until dry and oil starts to appear around the edges of the meat. Break cauliflower into florets and add to meat, cooking over low heat for 5 to 7 minutes. Add minced ginger, garlic, black pepper, and peas. Continue cooking until cauliflower and peas are tender but still crisp. Add coriander, cumin, *garam masala*, and chilies. Cook a few minutes and garnish with cilantro. Serve hot.

FISH CURRY
(Machha Ko Tarkari)

2 medium onions
1½ tbsp oil
15-oz can whole tomatoes
chilies and salt to taste
1 tsp garlic, minced

½ inch ginger, minced
1 tsp ground cumin
1 tsp ground coriander
two 15-oz cans fish (mackerel)
fresh cilantro, chopped

Fry onions in oil in a saucepan, stirring until onions are soft and half-cooked. Add canned tomatoes and cook for 5 minutes. Add chilies, salt, garlic, ginger, cumin, and coriander. Simmer for 15 minutes and add canned fish. Garnish with cilantro.

PRAWN CURRY
(Jhinge Machha Ko Tarkari)

3 tbsp oil
1 large onion, chopped
4 green chilies, chopped
1 tsp ground red chili
2 medium-size tomatoes, chopped
1 tsp fresh ginger, ground or minced

salt to taste
2 cloves garlic, minced
$\frac{1}{2}$ cup tamarind juice (thick)
$1\frac{1}{2}$ lb large prawns, shelled and washed
$\frac{1}{4}$ cup fresh cilantro, chopped
1 tbsp *garam masala*

Heat oil in a medium-size saucepan, and brown onion and green chilies. Add red chilies, tomatoes, ginger, salt, garlic, and tamarind juice. Simmer for 10 minutes. Add prawns, and cook for 10 minutes over medium heat. Sprinkle in cilantro and *garam masala*. Serve with plain rice.

CHICKEN DRUMSTICKS
(Kukhura Ko Khutta)

2 lbs chicken drumsticks
2 tbsp cooking wine
1 tbsp vegetable oil
1 tsp garlic powder

1 tsp ground cumin
$^2/_3$ tsp salt
$1^1/_2$ tsp ground red chili
1 tbsp soy sauce

Marinate chicken in a sauce made from the remaining ingredients, and leave it covered in the refrigerator for 4 hours. Preheat oven to 350°F and bake chicken for 1 hour. Turn drumsticks once after 45 minutes.

CHICKEN CHOW CHOW
(Kukhura Ko Chow Chow)

1 tbsp soy sauce
1 tsp vinegar
1 inch fresh ginger, minced
2 green chilies, chopped
1 tsp sugar
salt to taste
3 tbsp oil
1 lb boned chicken, cut in thin
   strips
³/₄ lb noodles
2 to 3 cups sliced mixed
   vegetables—mushrooms,
   bamboo shoots, carrots,
   French beans, etc.

1 bunch scallions
1 cup bean sprouts
1 hard-boiled egg

Sauce
2 tbsp soy sauce
1 tsp sugar
1 tsp vinegar
1 tbsp cornstarch
salt to taste
¹/₂ cup water

Make a marinade from the soy sauce, vinegar, ginger, green chilies, sugar, salt, 1 tablespoon of oil, and ¹/₂ cup water. Mix well and put in chicken. Let it stand for 15 minutes.

Boil noodles according to the packet instructions.

Heat 2 tablespoons oil in a pan and fry the chicken until tender. Add mixed vegetables, scallions, sprouts, and ¹/₂ cup boiling water. Simmer for 3 to 4 minutes.

Make a sauce from soy sauce, sugar, vinegar, cornstarch, salt, and water. Add to the chicken and vegetables, and simmer for another 3 to 4 minutes. Pour over noodles, and garnish with strips of boiled egg.

PORK CURRY
(Bangur Ko Tarkari)

3 lbs boneless, lean pork, cut
  into 1½-inch cubes
2 cloves garlic
2 bay leaves
1½ inches cinnamon stick
2 cloves

salt to taste
oil
2 medium onions, thinly sliced
3 green chilies
3 medium tomatoes, quartered
1 tsp ground cumin

Heat water in a large pan, add pork, garlic, bay leaves, cloves, cinnamon, and salt. Boil for ½ hour covered. Drain.

Heat the oil in a heavy saucepan and fry the pork until it is golden brown. Add onions, green chilies, tomatoes, and cumin, and cook until onions and tomatoes are soft, stirring occasionally.

MARINATED LAMB KABOB
(Muchhe Ko Khasi Ko Kabab)

2 tbsp vegetable oil
1/4 cup plain yogurt
2 tbsp tomato paste
2 tbsp lemon juice
1 medium onion, chopped
1/2 inch fresh ginger, chopped
4 cloves garlic, chopped
3/4 tsp each ground cumin, coriander, and pepper
1/2 tsp nutmeg

1/4 tsp mace
1/4 tsp turmeric
salt to taste
pinch of sugar
1 lb boneless lamb, fat trimmed, cut into 1-inch chunks
2 green peppers, cut into 1-inch pieces
wooden skewers

Blend all the above ingredients (except the peppers and lamb) in a blender to make a fine paste. Mix with the lamb pieces in a bowl, and cover and marinate overnight in the refrigerator.

Arrange lamb and green-pepper pieces alternately on skewers. Place skewers on a roasting rack in microwave at medium, or 50% of the capacity of microwave, for 9 to 12 minutes. Turn once after half the time. Serve warm.

SPICED ALMOND CHICKEN
(Masaledar Badami Kukhura)

8 small chicken breasts on the
  bone
juice of 1½ lemons
2 tsp salt
1 tsp cayenne pepper

Marinade:
½ cup raisins
⅔ cup flaked almonds
1 tbsp clear honey
2 cloves fresh garlic, chopped
2-inch piece fresh ginger,
  chopped

½ tsp ground cardamom
½ tsp cumin seeds
1 tsp turmeric
⅔ cup yogurt
½ cup cream

To cook chicken:
¼ tsp saffron threads, soaked
  in 2 tbsp boiling water for
  10 minutes
½ cup butter, melted

Remove skin from chicken, and make diagonal slits in each breast. In a small bowl, combine the lemon juice, salt, and cayenne, and rub this mixture all over the chicken, especially into the slits. Put the chicken breasts side by side in a shallow dish. Set aside for 30 minutes.

To make the marinade, put the raisins, almonds, honey, garlic, ginger and spices into a blender with 4 tablespoons of yogurt, and blend into a smooth puree. Transfer the puree to a bowl and beat in the remaining yogurt and cream. Pour over the chicken, cover, and chill in the refrigerator for 24 hours, turning the chicken breasts occasionally. The next day, remove the marinated chicken from the refrigerator and let it stand at room temperature for 1 hour.

To cook, drain and reserve the marinade, and arrange the chicken in a deep roasting pan. Combine the saffron mixture with the reserved marinade and pour it over the chicken. Spoon a little of the melted butter over the top. Roast the chicken in a preheated 400°F oven for 30 minutes, or until tender, basting frequently with the remaining melted butter and the liquid in the pan. If the marinade starts to dry out, add a small quantity of water. Transfer the chicken to a warmed serving dish. Spoon the pan juices over the chicken and serve.

CHICKEN CUTLETS
(Kukhura Chop)

1 tbsp fresh ginger, chopped
3 small cloves garlic, coarsely
    chopped
1 medium onion, finely
    chopped
3 green chilies (optional)
juice of 1 small lemon

salt to taste
1 lb chicken breasts, bone
    removed, cut into small, flat
    pieces
1 medium egg, beaten
bread crumbs
oil for frying

Place ginger, garlic, onion, chilies, lemon juice, and salt in a blender and make a paste. Pour over chicken and marinate overnight in refrigerator. Lift out chicken pieces, dip in egg, and coat both sides with bread crumbs; then fry in oil until golden brown. Serve warm.

SPANISH CHICKEN AND RICE
(Spanish Kukhura Bhat)

2 lbs chicken pieces
2 tsp dried oregano
$\frac{1}{2}$ tsp pepper
2 tsp salt
$\frac{1}{2}$ cup vegetable oil
1 medium green pepper
2 cups onion, chopped

2 cloves garlic, crushed
2 to 3 dried red chilies
1 bay leaf
2 cups washed raw rice
15-oz can crushed tomatoes
1 can chicken broth
2 cups frozen green peas

Wash chicken pieces under cold running water, and drain well; pat dry with paper towels. Combine oregano, pepper, and 1 teaspoon salt, then sprinkle mixture over chicken, rubbing well into skin. Let stand 5 to 10 minutes.

In a heavy Dutch oven, heat oil over medium heat. Brown chicken, a third at a time, until golden brown all over. Total time needed is about 30 minutes. Remove chicken as it browns. Preheat oven to 350°F.

Wash and dice green pepper. Add to drippings in Dutch oven with onion, garlic, whole red chilies, and bay leaf. Sauté, stirring over medium heat until golden. Add a little extra cayenne (red pepper) if you want it hotter.

Add 1 teaspoon salt and washed, drained rice. Cook, stirring until rice is lightly browned, about 10 minutes. Add undrained tomatoes and chicken broth and 1$\frac{1}{2}$ cups water. Arrange browned chicken pieces over rice mixture. Bring to boil uncovered. Immediately remove from stovetop and bake in oven, tightly covered, for 1 hour. Sprinkle peas over top and bake uncovered for another 20 minutes. Add $\frac{1}{2}$ cup water if needed.

NEPALI-STYLE QUAIL
(Battain Ko Tarkari)

4 to 6 small quail (frozen box from Manchester Farms, which can be bought in any grocery store)
1 tbsp ground cumin
1 tsp cinnamon
1 tsp ground cardamom
1/4 tsp ground cloves
1 tsp turmeric
1 tbsp fresh ginger, chopped
1 tbsp garlic, coarsely chopped
1 tsp salt, or to taste
1/2 cup water
1/4 cup mustard oil or other vegetable oil
1/2 tsp cumin seeds
1/2 tsp lovage seeds
1 dried red pepper
1 medium onion, finely sliced
1/2 cup fresh cilantro, chopped

Wash the quail carefully and cut into medium pieces.

In a small bowl, combine ground cumin, cinnamon, cardamom, cloves, turmeric, ginger, garlic, salt, and 1/2 cup water to make a paste.

Heat oil in a heavy saucepan over medium heat and add cumin seeds, lovage seeds, and red pepper. Cook until seeds pop, taking care not to burn the whole spices. Add sliced onions, stirring frequently, until they are golden brown. Add the spice paste and fry with the onions until their color darkens and oil appears around the edges. Add the quail pieces and stir well. Cook until brown. Add 1/2 cup water and cook for 25 minutes or until quail becomes tender. Add cilantro, cover, and simmer 5 minutes longer. Serve with rice.

HOT SPICY FISH
(Masala Machha)

1½ lbs fish steaks (trout is recommended), fresh if possible
1 medium onion, finely diced
1 tsp garlic, diced
1½ tsp fresh ginger, diced
2 fresh green chilies, seeded and chopped
1 small ripe tomato, peeled and chopped
½ tsp black pepper
2 tsp salt, or to taste
2 tbsp lemon juice
oil for frying
6 bay leaves
3 cardamom pods, bruised
1 small stick cinnamon
1 medium onion, finely sliced
1 cup yogurt

Wash fish, cut into serving pieces, and place in a large dish in layers.

In a blender, puree diced onion, garlic, ginger, chilies and tomato. Mix in black pepper, 1 teaspoon salt, and lemon juice, and pour over fish. Marinate for 15 minutes. Drain fish from marinade, reserving marinade.

Heat oil in a pan and fry fish pieces until golden brown on both sides.

In another pan, heat 1 tablespoon of oil and fry bay leaves, cardamom, cinnamon, and sliced onion until golden brown. Add reserved marinade, stir, and cook 5 minutes; then mix with yogurt. Gently add fish pieces and simmer 10 minutes over slow heat. Serve with rice.

BARBECUED PORK SPARERIBS
(Bandel Ko Karang)

2 cups chopped onion
1 cup ketchup
$\frac{1}{2}$ cup brown sugar, packed
2 tbsp curry powder
2 tsp paprika
1 tsp dry mustard

1 tsp Worcestershire sauce
1 tbsp hot pepper sauce
$\frac{1}{2}$ cup white vinegar
8 lbs spareribs
salt and pepper to taste
$\frac{1}{4}$ cup fresh lemon juice

In a saucepan, combine onion, ketchup, sugar, seasonings and vinegar; simmer for 10 to 15 minutes.

Rub salt and pepper into ribs and place them in a shallow roasting pan, meaty side down.

Brush ribs with the sauce and bake in a 400°F oven for 30 minutes. Turn the ribs, brush with more sauce and lemon juice. Bake another 15 minutes.

Keep in refrigerator, and when time to serve cook several minutes in charcoal grill.

FRIED CHICKEN GIZZARD
(Tara Ko Gizzard)

4 lbs chicken gizzards
⅓ cup oil
2 tbsp ground cumin
2 tbsp ground coriander
1 tsp turmeric

2 tbsp fresh ginger, finely
 chopped
10 cloves garlic, chopped
2 tbsp fresh cilantro

Heat oil in large saucepan over medium high heat. Fry ginger and garlic until lightly browned. Add gizzards and fry for 5 minutes. Stir in all spices and cook over medium heat, covered, until tender. Uncover and cook for 10 more minutes until it becomes dark brown and crispy. Garnish with cilantro.

CHICKEN FRIED RICE
(Khukara Ko Polau)

2 cups long grain or Basmati
  rice
1 ½ cups chicken breast, cut
  into small pieces
3 tbsp clarified butter
1 cardamom pod
2 cloves

2 bay leaves
1 medium onion, chopped
1 ½ tsp salt, or to taste
⅓ tsp turmeric
2 cloves garlic, chopped
1 tsp *garam masala*
2 cups water

Cover rice with water and allow to soak while cooking chicken.

Heat the clarified butter in a heavy skillet over medium high heat and fry cardamom, cloves and bay leaves until very light brown. Add chopped onion and cook, stirring, until golden brown. Add chicken, increase the heat to high, and fry until chicken is golden brown. Add salt, turmeric, garlic, ginger, and *garam masala*. Cook, covered, for 15 minutes.

Drain the rice and add to chicken. Fry until the rice is slightly browned. Pour in water, cover, and cook over medium heat for 10 more minutes.

TUNA-POTATO CUTLET
(Alu Ra Macha Ko Chop)

2 six-oz cans of water-base
  tuna fish, drained
2 lbs potatoes, boiled and
  mashed
1 tsp *garam masala*
1 tsp ground red chili

3 tbsp fresh cilantro, chopped
1 clove garlic, chopped fine
1 cup flavored bread crumbs
2 eggs
oil for deep frying

Mix tuna, mashed potato and spices, garlic and cilantro, and shape into patties. Beat eggs in a bowl. Dip patties in egg and then in bread crumbs. Heat oil and deep fry until brown. Serve hot with chutney, ketchup, or salsa

LAMB CURRY
(Khasi Ko Masu)

3 lbs lamb
2 tsp vegetable oil
2 cloves
$1/2$ tsp garlic powder
2 medium onions, sliced
$1/2$ tsp ground ginger
1 tsp ground cumin
$1/2$ tsp ground red chili
$1/4$ tsp nutmeg
1 tsp ground coriander

$1/2$ tsp turmeric
1 tsp salt (or to taste)
$1/2$ cup yogurt
1 medium tomato, cut into 8 pieces
$1/4$ tsp cinnamom
2 cardamon pods
$1 1/2$ cups water
2 tbsp fresh cilantro, chopped

Cut lamb into pieces. Heat oil in saucepan and add cloves, garlic and onion. Fry over low heat until lightly brown. Add ginger, cumin, chili, nutmeg, coriander, tumeric, and salt. Stir for 2 minutes, then add meat. Toss so that meat will be covered with spices. Cover and simmer for 30 minutes. Add yogurt, tomato, cinnamon, cardamom, and water. Cover and cook over medium heat for 5 minutes to allow sauce to thicken. Add cilantro just before serving. Serve with rice or poori (page 122).

The Bhaktapur, Durbar Square

CHUTNEYS AND PICKLES

TWICE-COOKED CHUTNEY
(Masala Ko Purano Achar)

4 tbsp red mustard seeds
4 tbsp cumin seeds
4 tbsp fenugreek seeds
4 tbsp lovage (*jwano*) seeds
4 tbsp szechwan pepper
1 cup vegetable oil
½ cup garlic cloves, halved
  lengthwise

½ cup fresh ginger, cut same
  size as garlic
1 tsp turmeric
1 cup ground red chili
salt to taste
16 oz lemon juice

Roast all the seeds together in a heavy pan. When cooled, grind them to a fine powder in a blender. Heat oil and fry garlic and ginger pieces 2 to 3 minutes or until golden brown. Add turmeric, ground chili, ground spices, and salt. Cook over medium heat, stirring constantly for 10 minutes. Add lemon juice and cook over low heat for 15 minutes, or until the mixture thickens to your liking. This chutney can be kept in the refrigerator for one year.

TOMATO AND CILANTRO CHUTNEY
(Golbheda Ra Dhania Ko Achar)

1 lb tomatoes
1 cup fresh cilantro, chopped
juice of ½ lemon
salt to taste
½ inch fresh ginger, chopped
4 cloves chopped garlic

½ tsp szechwan pepper
1 tsp ground red pepper
1 tbsp vegetable oil
¼ tsp fenugreek seeds
¼ tsp *jimbu*
pinch of asafetida

Wash and bake tomatoes in the oven at 450°F for 30 minutes, or until they look cooked and the skins turn dark. Blend baked tomatoes in a blender together with cilantro, lemon juice, salt, ginger, garlic, szechwan pepper, and red pepper. Heat oil and fry the asafetida, fenugreek, and *jimbu* until they turn black. Stir into the tomato paste mixture.

GRILLED TOMATO AND DRIED SHRIMP CHUTNEY
(Poleko Golbheda Ra Jhinge Machha Ko Achar)

½ lb tomatoes (preferably cherry or Italian plum tomatoes)

4 green chili peppers, grilled, sliced, and seeded

1 tbsp lemon juice

½ tsp minced garlic

½ tsp fresh ginger, minced

½ tsp cayenne pepper (or to taste)

¼ tsp szechwan pepper

salt to taste

½ cup oil for frying

½ cup dried shrimp, soaked in water for 5 minutes and drained

¼ cup fresh cilantro, chopped, for garnish

Broil the tomatoes under the grill, as close to the flame as possible. (A toaster oven also works well.) When the tomatoes are half done, place the green chilies in with tomatoes under the grill. Cook until the tomatoes are soft and the skins become dark.

Put cooked tomatoes, chilies and all other ingredients except the shrimp, oil and cilantro in a blender and grind quickly. (Do not over grind.) Put chutney in a serving bowl.

In a midsize saucepan, heat oil until it starts to smoke. Add shrimp and fry until crisp but not burned. Add the shrimp to the chutney just before serving and garnish with cilantro.

RHUBARB CHUTNEY
(Rhubarb Ko Achar)

1 lb rhubarb
1 tbsp oil
1/4 tsp fennel seeds
1/4 tsp black cumin seeds
1/4 tsp fenugreek seeds
1/4 tsp cumin seeds

1/2 tsp turmeric
1 tsp salt
1/4 cup sugar, or to taste
1/4 cup ground red chili
1/2 tsp ground cardamom
1/2 tsp ground cinnamon

Wash rhubarb and cut into small pieces. In a saucepan, heat oil and add fennel, black cumin, fenugreek, and cumin seeds, and let them brown over medium heat. Add the rhubarb, turmeric, and salt. After the rhubarb softens, add the sugar and chili powder; and cook for 10 minutes, stirring frequently. The rhubarb should soften completely. Add the cardamom and cinnamon, and cook for another 5 minutes. Cool and store in refrigerator in a glass jar.

CELERY AND POTATO PICKLE
(Celery Ra Alu Ko Achar)

4 cups of diced celery greens and hearts combined
1 tsp ground red chili
6 or 7 small, white, new potatoes—boiled, peeled and cut in half
1 tsp turmeric
1/4 cup sesame seeds, roasted and ground
juice of 1 lime or lemon

1/2 tsp ground szechwan pepper (optional)
salt to taste
1/8 tsp asafetida
1/2 cup cold water
4 tbsp mustard (or corn) oil
1/2 tsp fenugreek or cumin seeds
3 to 4 dried red (or green) chili peppers

Steam celery until tender. Mix all the ingredients except the oil, fenugreek seeds, and chilies in a big bowl. Add 1/2 cup cold water and mix well. Add more salt or lime juice according to taste. Heat the oil in a small pan. Add the fenugreek seeds to the hot oil and fry until they become dark. Add red or green peppers (or both) and continue frying until the red peppers become dark or green peppers become soft. Pour this fried mixture into the pickle bowl and mix well.

GINGER PICKLE
(Adua Ko Achar)

¼ to ⅓ lb ginger root
pulp of 1 cup tamarind (*see below*)
3 tbsp oil
½ cup whole red peppers
1 tbsp fenugreek seeds
1½ tbsp coriander seeds

1 tbsp cumin seeds
1½ tsp mustard seeds
6 to 8 cloves garlic
⅔ cup boiled water
2 tbsp salt
½ tsp szechwan pepper
fresh cilantro, finely chopped

Peel ginger and cut into small pieces.

To make tamarind pulp, boil 1 cup tamarind in ½ cup water for 5 minutes. Mash the cooled tamarind with a fork to release a pulpy paste. Strain the paste through a cheesecloth or fine sieve. Discard the seeds and fibers.

In a separate saucepan, heat oil and fry whole red peppers until light brown, approximately 1 minute. Remove from oil, drain, and set aside.

In the same pan fry fenugreek, coriander, and mustard seeds for 1 minute, then add garlic cloves and cook another minute. Drain seeds and garlic. Combine them with salt, szechwan pepper, red peppers, ginger, and tamarind pulp in a blender or food processor. Process to a smooth paste. Add finely chopped cilantro. Cool and store in refrigerator in a glass jar.

GREEN MANGO CHUTNEY
(Hario Aanp Ko Achar)

3 lb green mangoes, peeled, halved, and pitted
5 tbsp salt
9 cups water
2¹/₄ cups (1 lb) sugar
2¹/₂ cups white wine vinegar

2 inches fresh ginger, chopped
6 cloves garlic, crushed
2 tbsp hot chili powder
1 cinnamon stick
1 cup pitted dates
1 cup raisins

Chop the mango flesh finely and put in a bowl. Add the salt and water. Cover and set aside in a cool place for 24 hours. Place sugar and vinegar in a large heavy-bottomed saucepan and bring to a boil, stirring until the sugar has dissolved. Strain the mangoes, discarding the juice, and add them to the sugar-vinegar syrup. Add the remaining ingredients and bring to a boil, stirring frequently. Reduce the heat and simmer, stirring occasionally, for about 1¹/₂ hours or until the chutney is very thick. Remove the cinnamon stick and ladle the chutney into warmed, sterilized jars. Seal the jars and store until required.

DRIED VEGETABLE GREENS AND SOYBEAN PICKLE
(Gundruk Ra Bhatmas Ko Achar)

1 tbsp oil

1 cup *gundruk* (see recipe, page 32)

¼ cup roasted soybeans

3 cherry tomatoes

1 tsp salt

2 red chili peppers

6 szechwan peppercorns

1 tbsp mustard oil

¼ tsp turmeric

Seasoning

1 tsp oil

¼ tsp fenugreek seeds

¼ tsp *jimbu*

2 green chili peppers, sliced

In a saucepan heat oil and add *gundruk,* frying it over medium heat for about ½ minute. Mix all the ingredients (except the seasoning) and blend in a blender for 2 minutes.

To make the seasoning, heat oil in a small saucepan for about 2 minutes, until it reaches the smoking point. Add the fenugreek seeds, roasting them until they pop. Then add the *jimbu,* followed immediately by the sliced chilies. Cook for a few seconds, then mix seasoning into the rest of the dish. Serve with rice and *urad dal* (black lentils).

DAIKON RADISH PICKLE
(Moola Thepe Achar)

1 cup grated daikon radishes
1 or 2 green chili peppers,
  thinly sliced
2 tbsp fresh lemon juice
$\frac{1}{4}$ tsp szechwan pepper
$\frac{1}{4}$ tsp turmeric
salt to taste

2 tbsp oil (preferably mustard
  oil)
1 or 2 dried red chili peppers,
  broken in half
$\frac{1}{4}$ tsp fenugreek or cumin
  seeds
$\frac{1}{4}$ cup fresh cilantro, chopped

Squeeze out all the juice from the grated radishes and combine them with the green chilies, lemon juice, szechwan pepper, turmeric, salt, and some of the cilantro and mix well. Let stand for 15 minutes. In a small saucepan, heat the oil until smoking and then add the fenugreek and red chilies and cook until they become dark. Immediately pour this over the radish mixture and mix thoroughly. Garnish with the remaining cilantro before serving.

MASHED EGGPLANT PICKLE
(Bhanta Ko Chokha)

2 large eggplants
4 whole dried red chilies
½ inch fresh ginger

salt to taste
4 tsp mustard oil

Preheat oven to 350°F. Poke the eggplants with a fork in two places, rub them with oil, then wrap them in aluminum foil. Bake for 45 minutes to 1 hour (eggplants should be soft when done).

Remove eggplants from the oven, unwrap, and let them stand for ½ hour. Remove the skin.

Finely grind the chilies, ginger, and salt. Mix the skinned eggplant, ground spice mixture, and mustard oil. Mix thoroughly. Serve with rice or bread.

GREEN TOMATO CHUTNEY
(Hario Golbheda Ko Achar)

2 lbs firm green tomatoes
5 cloves garlic
1¹/₂ inches fresh ginger
12 oz white vinegar

1 lb brown sugar
1¹/₂ to 2 tsp ground red chili
1 tbsp salt
1¹/₂ tsp *garam masala*

Rinse, dry, and cut the tomatoes into small pieces; mince the garlic and ginger. Place the tomatoes, garlic, and ginger in a heavy (preferably non-stick) saucepan, and add the rest of the ingredients. Cook over medium heat for 55 minutes, stirring frequently and crushing the tomatoes slightly after they have become soft. Remove from heat and cool thoroughly before putting into a jar. Store in refrigerator.

ONION PICKLE
(Pyaj Ko Achar)

2 medium-size onions, sliced into thin lengthwise crescents
1 tsp salt, or to taste
2 tbsp sesame seeds, roasted and ground
$\frac{1}{4}$ tsp turmeric

$\frac{1}{4}$ tsp cayenne pepper
$1\frac{1}{2}$ tsp lime juice
pinch of szechwan pepper
2 tbsp mustard oil
$\frac{1}{4}$ tsp fenugreek or cumin seeds
2 dried red chilies

Sprinkle $\frac{1}{2}$ teaspoon salt onto the onions and let them stand in a bowl for 15 to 20 minutes, or until the onions start to wilt. Then squeeze the liquid from the onions. Add all ingredients except the oil, fenugreek, and red chilies, and mix well.

Heat the oil in a small pan until it smokes, then add the fenugreek and let it brown. Add red chili peppers and fry for a few seconds. Immediately pour this over the onion mixture and serve.

ROASTED SESAME SEED AND CILANTRO CHUTNEY
(Dhaniya Ra Til Ko Achar)

½ cup sesame seeds, dry-roasted and ground

1 cup fresh cilantro, chopped

7 or 8 fresh green chili peppers (for hot chutney) *or* 1 bell pepper, chopped, and ground red chili to taste

juice of 1 lemon or lime (or to taste)

2 cloves garlic

salt to taste

¼ tsp szechwan pepper

Combine all ingredients in a blender and grind them until smooth. Chill in the refrigerator before serving. This is an excellent dip with any kind of appetizer, especially mo-mos (pages 18-20) and samosas (see Potato-filled Pastries, page 27).

CAULIFLOWER AND GREEN CHILI PICKLE

(Kauli Ra Khursani Ko Achar)

1 cup cauliflower, cut into small pieces
2 cups boiled water, cooled
2 tbsp garlic, finely chopped
2 tbsp fresh ginger, finely chopped
2 tbsp mustard seeds, ground
5 tbsp fenugreek seeds, dry-roasted and ground

1 tsp ground red chili
4 tsp salt, or to taste
1 tbsp ground coriander
1 tsp turmeric
1 cup green chilies, chopped
$\frac{1}{2}$ cup mustard oil

Dry the cauliflower (traditionally done by spreading it on a clean towel and placing it in the sun for 6 hours or more). Mix the water and spices in a bowl with a wooden spoon. Add the cauliflower and green chilies, and then stir in the oil. Pour the mixture into a wide-mouth jar. Cover the mouth of the jar with plastic wrap. Keep the container in the sun for 3 to 4 days until the contents go sour, then keep inside at room temperature. Shake the container once a day. The pickle will be ready to eat in about two weeks and should be refrigerated once it has fermented. This pickle will keep for months in the refrigerator.

POTATO PICKLE
(Alu Ko Achar)

8 to 10 small, new red potatoes
3/4 cup sesame seeds, dry-roasted and ground
1 1/2 tbsp salt, or to taste
1/2 tsp ground red chili (optional)
juice of 2 1/2 lemons (or 1 tbsp tamarind pulp soaked in 2 tbsp water; use liquid only)
4 tbsp of mustard oil or any vegetable oil

4 to 5 fresh green chilies, seeded and thinly sliced
1/2 tsp fenugreek seeds
1/2 tsp turmeric
1/2 tsp *jimbu*
1/8 tsp asafetida
1/2 cup water
1/4 cup fresh cilantro, chopped

Boil and peel potatoes. Cut into quarters or cubes. Mix with sesame powder, salt, ground red chili, and lemon juice, stirring well. In a heavy saucepan with a lid, heat the oil and add green chilies. Fry until peppers are soft, then remove from the oil and mix with potatoes. Reheat the oil and fry the fenugreek until it is dark brown. Mix in the turmeric, *jimbu*, and asafetida. Pour mixture over potatoes and add the water and cilantro. Mix thoroughly and serve with plain rice.

Alu achar *is the most common* achar, *or pickle dish, served with Nepali meals. It is a semi-moist dish which goes well with rice, chicken, or fish. Alu achar looks and tastes more like a vegetable dish than other pickles.*

RAISIN PICKLE
(Dakh Ko Achar)

2 cups raisins
1 tbsp lemon juice
1 tsp salt
1 tbsp sugar
3 tbsp sesame seeds, dry-
  roasted and ground

dash of szechwan pepper
2 tbsp oil
3 pinches whole cumin seeds
1 pinch *jimbu*

Soak raisins in water until plump and tender. Drain off water and add lemon juice, salt, sugar, ground sesame, and szechwan pepper, mixing well. Heat oil in a small saucepan and add cumin; when the cumin turns golden brown, add *jimbu*. Remove from heat and pour on top of the raisins. Serve cool.

CABBAGE PICKLE
(Banda Ko Achar)

½ cup brown sesame seeds
¼ cup water
juice of 1 lemon or lime
½ medium-size cabbage,
   shredded (2½ cups)

1 tsp salt
½ tsp ground red chili
2 tbsp oil
¼ tsp turmeric

Roast the sesame seeds in a dry pan, stirring constantly until golden brown. Grind the seeds in a blender; then add water and lemon juice and blend into a paste. Mix sesame paste, shredded cabbage, salt, and ground chili. Heat the oil in a small pan over high heat until it smokes. Add turmeric to the hot oil and immediately pour it over the cabbage, mixing well. Add more salt, chili, and lemon juice to suit your taste.

HOT TOMATO PICKLE
(Piro Golbheda Ko Achar)

2 tbsp oil
salt to taste
6 cloves garlic, finely chopped
1½ inches fresh ginger, thinly
   sliced

5 to 6 medium-size fresh
   tomatoes, chopped
8 to 10 green chilies, sliced
   into diagonal strips

Put oil in a heavy skillet over medium heat and sprinkle with salt. Add garlic and ginger, cooking until they are light golden brown. Add tomatoes, sliced chilies, and more salt if necessary. Cover and cook slowly until tomato becomes a thick sauce.

CUCUMBER PICKLE
(Kankro Ko Achar)

4 cucumbers, peeled
1 tsp salt
$1/2$ cup brown sesame seeds
$1/4$ cup water

juice of 1 lemon or lime
$1/2$ tsp ground red chili
2 tbsp oil
$1/2$ tsp turmeric

Cut cucumbers into thirds, and then cut each third in half lengthwise. Remove seed section and slice into thin strips. Sprinkle with $1/2$ teaspoon salt and let stand for 1 hour.

Squeeze excess water from cucumbers. Add sesame paste, remaining salt, and chili powder, mixing well.

Roast the sesame seeds in a dry pan, stirring constantly until golden brown. Grind the sesame seeds in a blender; then add water and lemon juice and blend into paste.

Heat the oil in a small pan over high heat until it smokes. Add turmeric to the hot oil and immediately pour over the cucumber mixture, stirring well.

SESAME SEED PICKLE
(Til Ko Achar)

½ cup brown sesame seeds
1 tbsp crushed red pepper
juice from 1 lemon

salt to taste
1 tbsp oil
½ tsp fenugreek seeds

Dry-roast sesame seeds in a pan and grind into powder. Add pepper, lemon juice, and salt, and make a thin paste. Heat oil and add fenugreek seeds, and cook until the seeds turn dark golden brown. Pour over the sesame paste, and stir thoroughly.

CUCUMBER AND YOGURT PICKLE
(Kankro Ra Dahi Ko Achar)

2 cucumbers
2 tsp salt (to rub into cucumber slices)
2 tbsp sesame seeds
1 tbsp mustard oil
1 cup plain yogurt

lemon juice to taste
$\frac{1}{4}$ tsp fenugreek seeds
$\frac{1}{2}$ tsp turmeric
2 fresh green chilies, seeded and thinly sliced
1 tbsp fresh cilantro, chopped

Peel the cucumbers, halve them lengthwise, and remove the seeds. Cut the cucumber into small slices. Sprinkle with salt and leave for 15 minutes.

Dry-roast sesame seeds, shaking pan or stirring constantly, until light brown; grind to powder form.

Drain liquid from cucumbers by pressing with two hands. Combine with yogurt, lemon juice, sesame powder, and turmeric. Taste to see if more salt is required. Heat oil, fry fenugreek seeds, and pour over cucumbers, mixing well.

FISH PICKLE
(Machha Ko Achar)

1 to 2 lb salmon or fish of
   choice
salt to taste
pinch of tartaric acid crystals

oil for deep frying
4 to 5 red chili peppers
2 tbsp coriander seeds
$\frac{1}{2}$ tsp turmeric

Cut fish into bite-size pieces and wash it thoroughly. Rub with salt and tartaric acid crystals (available in Indian grocery stores), and let it stand at room temperature for at least one hour. Drain the fish in a colander and then deep fry it until golden brown.

In a small frying pan roast chili pepper and coriander seeds, then grind them together with salt, a pinch of tartaric acid, and turmeric. Pour the ground spices over the fried fish and mix thoroughly.

Easy Tomato Pickle
(Golbheda Ko Achar)

1 can whole tomatoes
green chilies, to taste
6 cloves crushed garlic

fresh cilantro, chopped, to
taste

Crush the tomatoes and mix all the ingredients thoroughly.

SESAME SEED AND SPINACH PICKLE
(Palungo Ko Achar)

1 lb fresh spinach, washed and
   broken into pieces
$^1/_4$ cup water
$^1/_4$ cup sesame seeds, dry-
   roasted and ground
$1^1/_2$ tbsp lemon juice
ground red chili and salt to
   taste

2 tbsp mustard oil
2-3 dried red chilies
$^1/_4$ tsp turmeric
10 fenugreek seeds
pinch of *jimbu* (optional)

Boil the spinach with $^1/_4$ cup water until soft. Squeeze out the water. Add ground sesame seed, lemon juice, chili powder and salt. Heat oil in a small frying pan. Add fenugreek seeds, whole chilies and *jimbu*, and cook until they turn black. Remove pan from heat and add turmeric. Add this to the spinach and mix well.

RICE AND BREADS

NEPALI CORN BREAD
(Makai Ko Roti)

3½ cups corn flour
1 tsp salt

1 cup hot water
2 tbsp clarified butter

Combine above ingredients, adding water all at once and mixing to make a firm but not stiff dough. Knead dough for at least 5 minutes. Form dough into a ball, cover with clear plastic wrap, and let stand for 1 hour or longer.

Divide the dough into balls (about the size of a medium potato). Roll the bread on a round wood disk (available in Indian groceries) or on a cutting board. Roll very carefully; otherwise it will break. To remove from the disk, put your hand softly on the bread and turn the disk a little, taking the bread on the palm.

Cook on a heavy non-stick pan over a slow heat until it is done on both sides. Put some clarified butter on both sides. Serve with any vegetable.

PLAIN WHEAT FLAT BREAD
(Sukkha Roti, or Chapati)

2 1/2 cups whole-wheat flour water
1/4 tsp salt butter

Mix 2 cups flour with salt and enough water to make a soft, pliable dough. Knead well (kneading keeps the bread light). Cover with a damp cloth and let sit for an hour or so. Knead well again. Break off into small pieces, form into balls, and roll each ball into a small pancake.

Heat a dry griddle over medium heat, and place the bread on it for 25 to 30 seconds, or until small bubbles appear on the surface of the bread. Then turn it over and cook it until brown spots appear. Turn again to the first side, and press the top gently with a cloth until the bread puffs up. Remove from the griddle, spread butter (if desired) on the top of the bread, and keep it covered with a cloth or kitchen towel before serving. Serve warm with curry, *dal*, or chutney.

Variation: The bread can be baked by placing it on the bottom rack of a preheated oven at 350°F. Allow it to puff up for 2 to 3 minutes.

FRIED PUFFED BREAD
(Poori)

1 cup whole-wheat flour
1 cup unsifted all-purpose
  flour
2 tsp salt

¼ cup shortening
¾ cup water (approximately)
oil for deep frying

In a large bowl combine flour and salt. Cut shortening into the flour, and mix until it resembles coarse meal. Add water and mix with a fork. Form dough into a ball. On a lightly floured surface, knead dough until it is smooth and elastic. Place dough ball in a bowl and cover it with a damp cloth; let it rest 15 minutes. (For the food processor method, use steel knife attachment of your processor. Place flour, salt, and shortening in bowl. Turn machine on and off until mixture resembles coarse meal. With machine running, add water gradually through feed tube until dough forms a ball. Allow processor to run for 3 minutes to knead dough.)

Form dough into small balls approximately 1 inch in diameter. On a lightly floured surface, roll out each ball to form a 4-to 5-inch circle. In a deep fryer heat 2 inches of oil to 375°F. Fry the bread, a few pieces at a time, until golden and puffed. Cook each side until crisp and light brown. Remove with slotted spoon and drain on paper towels. Makes 20 pieces. Serve immediately with meat or vegetables.

FLAKY WHEAT BREAD, OR ROTI
(Parautha)

2 cups whole-wheat flour
$1/4$ tsp salt
water

$1/4$ cup melted clarified
butter or shortening

Mix flour and salt, and add enough water to make a stiff dough. Knead well (at least 5 minutes). Cover with a damp cloth and let stand for one hour. Knead well again. Break the dough into small pieces, form into balls, and roll each into a very thin circle. Brush each circle with melted clarified butter or shortening and fold over into a semicircle. Brush again and fold again into a quarter circle, or fold from both sides to form a small square. Roll the quarter circle or square into a thin circle to the size of a small plate. Heat griddle or iron skillet and brush lightly with clarified butter or shortening. Fry each *parautha* until brown and crisp on both sides, turning frequently and adding more butter around the edges so the bread will be flaky and crisp. Serve hot with curry.

RICE FLAKE PILAF
(Chiura Ko Pulau)

2 tbsp oil or butter
1 bay leaf
1 small onion, chopped
1 medium potato, peeled and
　cubed
¹/₂ medium-size cauliflower,
　cut into small pieces
1 tsp salt

¹/₄ tsp turmeric
¹/₂ tsp ground cumin
¹/₄ tsp ground coriander
ground red chili to taste
¹/₂ cup green peas
2 cups rice flakes
¹/₄ tsp *garam masala*
1 tbsp fresh cilantro, chopped

Heat oil in a heavy, preferably non-stick, saucepan. Fry the bay leaf and onion until the onion becomes golden brown. Add the potato and cook for 2 minutes, then add the cauliflower and cook for 3 to 4 minutes. Add the salt and other spices except cilantro and *garam masala*. Cook covered over medium-low heat for 5 minutes and then add the peas; cook 5 more minutes. Wash rice flakes in cold water and drain well. Immediately mix it with the vegetables and cook for 10 minutes, covered, over low heat. Just before taking it off the heat, sprinkle with *garam masala* and cilantro. Serve hot.

RICE SALAD
(Saden Ko Bhat)

3 cups cooked rice (refrigerated prior to use)
1 medium tomato, chopped
$^1/_2$ cup boiled sweet corn or canned chickpeas
1 cup shredded lettuce
$^1/_2$ cup raw cashew nuts (optional)

3 tbsp mustard oil or salad oil
1 clove garlic, minced
$^1/_2$ tsp ground red chili or black pepper
$^1/_4$ cup cilantro or parsley, minced
salt to taste

Mix all the ingredients together in a big bowl with wooden spatula. This is an excellent side dish with all kinds of barbecued meats.

PLAIN RICE
(Sada Bhat)

2 cups long grain or *Basmati*
  rice
4 cups water
1 tsp unsalted butter (optional)

Wash rice and soak for 5 minutes. Boil the rice over medium-high heat for 10 minutes. Stir once thoroughly. If desired, add 1 teaspoon butter to make rice soft and fluffy. Turn the heat to low and cook, covered, for 5 more minutes

CORNMEAL PORRIDGE
(Makai Ko Dhindo)

4 cups water
2 cups clarified butter
salt to taste

1 cup corn flour
1 cup coarse cornmeal

Boil water with the butter and salt in a thick-bottomed saucepan or cast iron pan (in Nepal an iron pan known as *tapke* is used). Mix corn flour and cornmeal. When water starts to boil, add cornmeal mixture, 1 to 2 tablespoons at a time, and stir vigorously with a wooden spatula after each addition. Continue adding cornmeal to the water, stirring constantly, until all the cornmeal is dissolved and the mixture is smooth. Cook until the porridge thickens and starts separating from the edges of the pan. Serve hot.

This dish comes from the farming people of the hilly regions of Nepal, who find it more filling and nutritious than the common staple diet of rice. Millet flour is sometimes substituted for corn flour. Dhindo *is eaten with vegetables, pickles, yogurt, and buttermilk.* Dhindo *and* Gundruk *(see page 32) together form the most typical food combination among the peasants in the Nepalese hill regions.*

FRIED RICE WITH PEAS
(Matar Ko Pulau)

1½ cups rice
3 tsp clarified butter
1 medium onion, finely
  chopped
1 tsp cumin seeds

2 green cardamom pods
2 cloves
½ cup green peas
salt to taste
3 cups hot water

Soak rice in water for 5 minutes, then drain. Heat butter and fry onions until brown. Add all the spices, and then the peas, and cook for a few minutes. Add the rice and salt, frying until the rice is dried and looks slightly brownish. Pour in the water, cover, and boil gently until the rice is tender.

NEPALI EGG BREAD
(Phool Roti)

4 medium eggs
1 cup all-purpose flour
$^1/_8$ tsp black pepper

salt to taste
$^1/_2$ cup water

Mix eggs, flour, black pepper, and salt thoroughly. Add water until the mixture has become the consistency of pancake batter. Pour a small amount of batter into a heated non-stick pan and and spread. It should be paper thin. Cook it until done. Serve with vegetables.

Hanuman, King of Monkeys

DESSERTS

HOMEMADE YOGURT
(Dahi)

1 gallon whole fresh milk
1 cup prepared yogurt (any
  plain yogurt culture)

Bring milk to a full boil, stirring occasionally with a spoon. Be careful not to burn it. Remove pan from heat and place in a refrigerator or in a sink of cold water to cool the milk. When milk has cooled to a little warmer than normal body temperature, add the yogurt culture. Stir and mix thoroughly. Yogurt culture tends to stay on the bottom of the pot, so stir carefully. Leave covered pan in warm place overnight until yogurt thickens (on top of a refrigerator, or in gas oven with pilot light, or another place to maintain temperature of 110°F.) If the yogurt is thin and watery, you should purchase fresh yogurt culture to use for starter.

FRIED NEPALI COOKIES
(Lakhamari)

2 cups all-purpose flour
1/2 cup shortening or clarified
  butter
2 cups warm water

oil for deep frying
1 1/2 cups sugar
1/2 cup water

Mix flour and shortening thoroughly for 5 minutes. Add water and mix the dough. Form into different shapes. Heat the oil in a saucepan and deep fry cookies over medium-low heat until golden brown.

Syrup

Boil 1 1/2 cups sugar in 1/2 cup water until it becomes sticky. Pour hot syrup over cookies until they are well coated.

CHICKPEA-FLOUR SWEETS
(Besan Ko Laddu)

1 cup unsalted butter
1¹/₂ cups sifted chickpea flour
1¹/₂ cups dry, shredded coconut
2 cups sugar
seeds of 8 cardamom pods,
   crushed

³/₄ cup unsalted almonds (or
   walnuts), chopped
2 tbsp pistachio nuts, chopped

Melt the butter in a frying pan, and add the chickpea flour little by little. Stir continually until the flour is roasted and turns slightly darker. Add the coconut and stir a bit longer. Remove from the heat and add the sugar, cardamom and nuts. Mix well. Let it cool until it can be handled comfortably. When cool enough to handle, divide the mixture into several parts, and squeeze into round balls about 1 inch in diameter.

NEPALI PEDA COOKIES
(Gokul Ko Peda)

1 cup heavy cream
2½ cups milk powder
¾ cup sugar

1 tsp ground cardamom
1 tsp saffron
2 tbsp pistachio nuts, sliced

Boil the cream in a heavy saucepan for 1 minute over medium heat. Lower the heat and add the milk powder. Stir until the cream becomes thick and leaves the sides of the pan. Mix in the sugar, cardamom, and saffron. After it cools, knead the dough vigorously. Make balls and then press flat between the palms of your hands. Garnish with a few pieces of sliced pistachio.

BAKED SOUR CREAM SQUARES
(Dahi Barfi)

2 pints sour cream
¼ tsp baking powder
9-oz can condensed milk

1 tbsp each almonds and
   cashews, chopped
1 tbsp golden raisins

Mix the sour cream, baking powder, and milk thoroughly. Mix in the almonds, cashews, and raisins, and spread in a baking dish. Bake for 15 to 20 minutes at 325°F until the sides start browning. Put in refrigerator to chill, then cut into small pieces and serve.

COCONUT FUDGE
(Naribal Ko Barfi)

1½ to 2 cups sugar (according
   to taste)
½ cup water

seeds of 6 cardamom pods,
   crushed
1 fresh coconut

Mix sugar, water, and cardamom in a heavy saucepan. Cook over medium heat until it turns to syrup. Break fresh coconut, remove brown skin, and grate the coconut meat by hand or in a food processor. Add grated coconut to syrup. Cool for 15 to 20 minutes until the syrup almost disappears into coconut. Spread the coconut mixture on a greased cookie sheet (use very little oil), smoothing out the top. Let it cool, and then cut into 1-inch square pieces.

SWEET YOGURT WITH SPICES
(Sikarni)

4 cups yogurt
$1/2$ tsp rose water
pinch of saffron
2 cups sugar

$1/2$ tsp ground cinnamon
$1/2$ tsp ground black pepper
$1/2$ tsp ground cloves

Place yogurt in cheesecloth to drain for 6 to 8 hours, depending on the consistency desired. Put the rose water and saffron in a small bowl, and let it stand for a while. Mix thoroughly so that the saffron gets dissolved in rose water. Add to the yogurt. Combine the sugar and spices, then add to the yogurt mixture. Stir for 5 minutes. Serve in small cups.

NEPALI PEDA COOKIES
(Peda)

1 gallon milk, for paneer
2 tbsp lemon juice
¼ lb unsalted butter
1 cup heavy cream

2 cups milk powder
sugar, to taste
1 tsp ground cardamom
2 tbsp pistachio nuts, sliced

To make peda cookies you will first need to make paneer, which is a kind of homemade cottage cheese. Begin by boiling the milk, preferably in a 5 quart non-stick pan. Stir in the lemon juice as soon as the milk begins to boil. Remove from heat when curds begin to separate from the milk. Cover and let sit for half an hour, or until it becomes solid. Strain through a cheesecloth, then tie the paneer into the cheesecloth and hang it up for about an hour so that it will drain. Finally, knead the paneer to make it smooth.

Fry paneer in butter for 5 minutes (frying will turn it into a paste). Let cool for 10 minutes, then add heavy cream and mix thoroughly. Add the cardamom and mix again, then add dry milk. Cook about 10 minutes over medium heat and then add sugar, stirring until well blended. Allow mixture to cool. When it becomes thick, form into small balls. Place ball in the palm of the left hand; with thumb make a well in middle and place in some sliced pistachio. Set in refrigerator to harden.

WHEAT-FLOUR PUDDING
(Manabhog)

1 cup whole-wheat flour
½ cup boiling water
¾ cup sugar
2 tbsp sweet butter

¼ cup raisins
¼ tsp ground cardamom
¼ cup raw almonds or cashew
  nuts, sliced

Brown flour lightly in a dry, deep heavy pan or wok over low heat. Add water gradually, stirring constantly to prevent lumps. Cook slowly over low heat until pudding becomes almost dry. Add sugar, butter, raisins, and cardamom. Stirring continuously, simmer for 5 minutes, or until the pudding starts to separate from the pan. Place in a serving dish and decorate with almonds or cashews. Serve hot, smothered in thick cream, if you wish.

CRISPY RICE DOUGHNUTS
(Sel)

2 cups rice (any kind)
2 tbsp clarified butter or
   shortening (optional)
1 small ripe banana
1 tsp milk (optional—add only
   to make soft doughnuts)

1 to 1$^1/_2$ cups sugar
pinch of baking soda
oil for deep frying

Soak rice overnight. Drain off the water, and then grind the rice, sugar, shortening, banana, and baking soda in a blender. If necessary, sprinkle a little water while grinding to form a smooth cream, but do not make it too fine. Heat oil in a deep frying pan, then pour in the batter using a small funnel (or a cloth icing bag with a medium-size opening.) Make circles like a doughnut. Fry turning once, until they are golden brown and crisp on both sides. Lift out on a slotted spoon and let the oil drain for a few seconds. Can be served hot or cold.

DESSERT CROISSANT
(Sajilo Goji)

Dough

1 cup sour cream
5 cups all-purpose flour

2 cups margarine

Mix ingredients in a large bowl. Chill overnight.

Filling

1½ cups chopped nuts
1 cup sugar

1 cup shredded coconut
2 tsp ground cinnamon

Mix the filling ingredients and set them aside. Divide the dough into 4 parts. Roll each part into a rectangle 15 by 12 inches wide. Cut into pieces using a 3-inch round cookie cutter. Fill each one with filling and shape like crescent. Bake on an ungreased cookie sheet at 375°F for 15 to 18 minutes. Cool.

Glaze

1 cup powdered sugar
½ cup water

½ cup shredded coconut

Make a syrup by mixing the sugar and water, and boiling 5 to 10 minutes. Spread a small amount of syrup on one side of each crescent and sprinkle with coconut. Makes about 75 croissants. Serve as a snack or dessert.

DESSERT BALLS IN SYRUP
(Gulab Jamun)

2 cups powdered milk
1 cup Bisquick
¼ cup unsalted butter
¾ cup milk
oil for deep frying

Syrup
2 cups white sugar
4 cups water
5 cardamom pods, bruised
2 tbsp rose water, or a few
    drops of rose essence

Mix together the Bisquick, powdered milk, and butter, and add enough milk to make a firm but pliable dough. Mold the dough into balls the size of large marbles.

Make the syrup by combining the sugar, water, and cardamom, and cooking for 5 to 10 minutes.

Heat the oil and fry the balls over low heat until they slowly turn golden brown. Lift out on a slotted spoon and drain on paper towel.

Put the fried balls into the warm syrup and add rose water. When they have cooled somewhat, the balls will swell and become spongy. Soak 12 hours in syrup. Serve at room temperature or chilled.

REKHA'S SWEET BALLS
(Pitho Ko Laddu)

3 cups unbleached flour
1 cup unsalted sunflower
  seeds

$^2/_3$ lb clarified butter
$^1/_2$ cup shredded coconut
$^1/_2$ cup sugar

Fry the flour in the butter over medium heat in a deep pan or wok until it is golden brown. Cool the thick paste mixture, then add the sugar, coconut, and sunflower seeds, mixing well. Shape into 1-inch balls. Makes 30 balls.

MANGO ICE CREAM CONES
(Aap Ko Kulfi)

1 cup mango slices in syrup
1 cup mango pulp
14-oz can sweetened
   condensed milk
1 cup heavy cream

2 cups milk
$1/4$ tsp pure vanilla extract
3 oz ground almonds or
   pistachios

Put mangoes with syrup and pulp into the container of a food processor. Blend to a fine puree. Add condensed milk. Add the cream and milk and blend well. Add vanilla extract. Pour into small cone-shaped molds and freeze. The consistency will be thicker and harder than ordinary ice cream, but it melts quickly and must be eaten within a few minutes.

NEPALI DOUGHNUTS
(Khajuri)

---

2 cups all-purpose flour
¼ cup sugar
¼ cup clarified butter
¼ tsp ground cardamom
¼ tsp ground cloves

shredded coconut and raisins
   to taste
¼ cup milk
oil for deep frying

Mix above ingredients with the milk. Shape like doughnuts and deep fry in shortening or butter.

SWEET CHICKPEA BALLS
(Bundi Laddu)

1½ cups chickpea flour
1 cup water
pinch of baking powder
½ tsp saffron, dissolved in 2
   tbsp warm water

10 cardamom pods, crushed
   fine
2 cups sugar
oil for deep frying
pistachio nuts, finely chopped

Make a thin batter of the chickpea flour and water. Add baking powder and half of the saffron water. Mix well and set aside.

Mix the cardamom, remaining saffron, sugar, and water, and cook down until it begins to crystallize on the sides of the pan. Keep the syrup warm.

Heat the oil. Put a spoonful of batter on a large-holed sieve and tap the batter into the hot oil, to form little crispy balls. Fry them quickly to a golden color. As the balls cook, put them into the thick syrup. When all the cooked batter has been put in syrup, let it cool for 1 hour. As it cools, the little balls become moist and stick together. Form into walnut-size balls. Decorate with finely chopped pistachios.

ALMOND FUDGE
(Badam Barfi)

2 cups almonds, blanched
2 tbsp unsalted butter
2 cups milk

seeds of 5 cardamom pods,
  crushed
³/₄ cup sugar

Grind almonds and cardamom in a blender until they become a fine powder. Bring milk to a boil and simmer for about 30 minutes, until it has the consistency of cream soup. Reduce heat, add sugar, and cook for 3 minutes. Add the powdered almond and the butter. Stir vigorously. Flatten and spread on a cookie sheet and cut into pieces.

RICE DUMPLINGS WITH SESAME SEEDS AND COCONUT
(Yamari)

2 cups rice flour
1 cup boiled water
1 cup sesame seeds, dry-
  roasted and ground

1 cup brown sugar
$^1/_2$ cup shredded coconut

Combine rice flour and hot water, mixing with a spoon until the dough can be handled easily. Knead the dough until it is soft and does not crack while rolling on palm. Cover dough with a moist cloth.

Process shredded coconut in a blender to make a fine powder. In a bowl, mix ground sesame, brown sugar, and coconut powder; stir thoroughly to make a paste.

Take a small quantity of dough and shape it into a hollow shape like an egg shell. Care should be taken not to break the wall. Spoon 1 tablespoon of sesame paste mixture into the shell and completely close the mouth of the dough. After a batch has been prepared, steam them in a steamer until they appear glazed. Serve warm with pickle or other side dish.

LEMON BREAD
(Kagati Kek)

1 cup butter, softened
1 cup sugar
3 eggs, separated
1 lemon rind, grated
3 cups all-purpose flour
2 tsp baking powder
¼ tsp salt
1 cup milk

1 cup chopped nuts (walnuts, pecans or hazelnuts)

Topping
2 tbsp butter, melted
1¼ cups powdered sugar
3 tbsp lemon juice
1½ tsp grated lemon rind

Preheat oven to 350°F. Grease and flour two 8" x 4" loaf pans. Cream butter and sugar until light and fluffy; beat in egg yolks and lemon rind. Stir together flour, baking powder, and salt, and add to butter mixture alternately with milk. Beat egg whites until stiff but not dry; fold into bread mixture along with nuts. Pour into two loaf pans; bake for 1 hour or until done. Combine topping ingredients and drizzle over cooled loaves.

SEMOLINA BALLS
(Suji Ko Laddu)

¹/₄ cup clarified butter
1 cup cream of wheat
5 to 6 cardamom pods
10 to 12 raisins
2 tbsp almonds or cashews,
   chopped

1 tbsp butter
¹/₄ cup milk
1 cup sugar
2 tbsp sweetened coconut

Melt the butter in a non-stick skillet and roast the cream of wheat over medium-low heat for 10 minutes, stirring constantly, until a nice aroma arises.

Crush cardamom into powder.

Fry raisins and nuts in a tablespoon of butter until golden brown; add these to the cream of wheat.

Boil the milk. Add a couple of spoonfuls of milk to the cream of wheat mixture and stir. Mix in the sugar, and then add the rest of the milk, the cardamom powder, and the coconut. Mix thoroughly. Form small portions of the mixture into balls. Makes about 18 medium-sized balls.

RICOTTA CHEESE SQUARES IN CREAM

(Ras Malai)

32 oz ricotta cheese
1½ cups sugar
32 oz half-and-half milk
½ tsp ground cardamom

1 tbsp rose water
2 tbsp pistachio nuts, finely
   chopped
pinch of saffron

Mix ricotta cheese and 1 cup sugar in a rectangular baking pan. Mash into paste with a fork and bake in a pre-heated oven at 325°F for 30 minutes. Cool, and cut into small squares.

While the ricotta mixture is in the oven, combine the half-and-half, ½ cup sugar, and cardamom in a pan and bring to a boil. Cook over medium heat for 15 minutes or until it thickens. When cooked, pour over the cooled ricotta pieces. Sprinkle with rose water, pistachio nuts, and saffron. Chill in the refrigerator.

CARROT FUDGE
(GAJAR KO BARFI)

2 cups half-and-half milk
1 pound carrots, grated in food
  processor
1 stick sweet butter
$^3/_4$ cup sugar

$^1/_2$ cup ground almonds
$^1/_4$ tsp ground cardamom
1 tbsp rose water
$^1/_2$ cup cashew nuts, chopped

Simmer carrots and half-and-half over medium heat for 45 minutes, stirring constantly. Add butter, sugar, almonds, cardamom, and rose water. Continue cooking over medium heat until the mixture thickens. Remove from heat and mix in cashews. Spread mixture in a buttered rectangular baking pan. Cool and cut into diamond-shaped pieces.

RICE PUDDING
(Khir)

1 gallon milk
1^1/$_2$ cups rice
2 tsp butter
^{1}/$_4$ cup shredded coconut
^{1}/$_4$ cup cashews, chopped

^{1}/$_4$ cup sugar, or to taste
^{1}/$_4$ cup raisins
3 or 4 cardamom pods

Bring milk to a boil in a big saucepan. Add rice and butter, stirring constantly for 2 minutes. Allow to simmer over low heat for 15 to 20 minutes. Then add coconut, cashews, sugar, raisins, and cardamom, and stir for 2 minutes. Cover and cook for another 5 to 10 minutes until rice is done.

SWEET BREAD
(Malpuwa)

2 cups all-purpose flour
1 cup sugar (or to taste)
3 tbsp shredded, unsweetened
  coconut
2 tbsp fennel seeds
¼ tsp ground black pepper

2 ripe bananas, mashed
1 cup milk
1 cup water
2 cups oil or clarified butter
  for frying

Mix all dry ingredients. In a separate bowl combine banana, milk and water, and slowly add to the dry ingredients until the mixture resembles pancake batter. Let stand at room temperature for one hour. Heat all of the oil or ghee in a frying pan over medium heat. Using two tablespoons of the batter at a time, form pancakes and deep-fry until golden. These can also be cooked like ordinary pancakes, using only a tablespoon of clarified butter or oil in the pan. Serve hot or cold.

MUNG BEAN FUDGE
(Mung Dal Ko Barfi)

4 tbsp clarified butter
1 lb mung beans (*mung dal*)
1 lb unsweetened *khuwa*
  (solidified milk) or milk
  powder
1½ cups sugar, or to taste
⅓ cup almonds, blanched and
  sliced

⅓ cup unsalted pistachio nuts,
  sliced
⅓ cup unsalted sunflower
  seeds (raw or roasted)
¼ tsp essence of rosewater
1 tsp ground cardamom
1½ cups water

Soak the mung beans overnight. Drain and grind to a paste in a blender.

In a medium-size non-stick pan, add water and sugar and cook syrup to a "one-thread" consistency. To test consistency, take a drop of cooled syrup between the thumb and index finger. Pull fingers apart, and when a single thread appears between the fingers, the syrup is done. Remove from heat and keep warm.

Heat the clarified butter in a non-stick pan, add the bean paste and cook over medium heat until golden in color. Add the dry milk and mix until smooth. Add the syrup, nuts, and cardamom and cook until the mixture becomes thick and leaves the sides of the pan. Add the rose water essence and remove from heat. Spread in a greased flat dish and cut into small squares.

SWEET YOGURT-PISTACHIO DESSERT
(Sikarni)

32-oz container of yogurt or
    yogurt made from 1 gallon
    of whole milk
1 tsp stem saffron
$^1/_2$ tsp water
1 cup sugar, or to taste

6 cardamom pods, finely
    ground
$^1/_2$ tsp ground nutmeg
$^1/_2$ cup shelled, unsalted
    pistachio nuts

Line a large colander with a double thickness of cheesecloth. Add yogurt, cover, and let it drain about 6 to 8 hours. The yogurt will give up a good deal of liquid and will thicken. Put the firm yogurt in a mixing bowl. Blend the saffron and water in a small mortar to make a paste. Add the saffron, sugar, cardamom, and nutmeg to the yogurt and blend thoroughly. Cut the pistachio nuts into thin slivers. Mix half of them into the yogurt and use half to garnish the top. Chill. This dessert will keep in the refrigerator for more than two weeks.

ENGLISH-NEPALI GLOSSARY

ENGLISH	NEPALI
Aniseed	Saunf
Asafetida	Hing
Asparagus	Kurilo
Bamboo Shoots	Tama
Baking Soda	Khane Soda
Bay Leaf	Tej Paat
Beet Roots	Chukander
Black Cumin	Mungrelo
Black-eyed Peas	Bodi (Sukeko)
Black Lentils	Maas or Urad
Bread	Roti
Brown Sugar	Sakkhar
Buckwheat	Phapar
Butter	Nauni or Makkhan
Cabbage	Banda Gobi
Cardamom (black)	Alaichi
Cardamom (green)	Sukumel
Carrot	Gajar
Cauliflower	Kauli
Cheese	Chij or Paneer
Chickpea	Chana
Chickpea or Gram Flour	Besan
Chili Pepper	Khorsani
Chive	Chyaapi
Chive (Chinese)	Dundu ko Saag
Cilantro, Chinese Parsley, or Green Coriander	Hario Dhaniya
Cinnamon	Dalchini

ENGLISH	NEPALI
Clove	Luang
Coriander Seeds	Dhaniya Geda
Corn	Makai
Cucumber	Kankro
Cumin	Jeera
Daikon Radish	Mula
Egg	Phul
Eggplant or Aubergine	Bhanta
Fava or Broad Bean	Bakula
Fava or Broad Bean (Green)	Bakula simi
Fenugreek	Methi
Flour	Pitho
Garlic	Lasun
Ginger (Fresh)	Adua
Ginger (Dry)	Sutho
Green Bean	Simi
Green Dill	Saunf ko Saag
Jimbu	Jimbu
Kohlrabi	Gyanth Gobi
Lentil	Dal
Lovage or Ommum	Jwanu
Mace	Jaipatri
Millet	Kodo
Garam Masala	Garam Masala
Molasses	Khudo
Mushroom	Chyau
Mustard Greens	Rayo ko Saag
Mustard Seeds (Dark)	Rayo, Tori
Mustard Seeds (Yellow)	Sarsyun
Nutmeg	Jaiphal
Oats	Jau
Okra or Lady's Finger	Ramtoriya
Peas (Green)	Hariyo Kerau/Matar
Pepper (Green or Red)	Khursani
Pepper (Bell)	Bhede Khursani
Pepper (Black)	Marich
Potato	Alu
Pumpkin	Pharsi

ENGLISH	NEPALI
Rice	
Beaten	Chiura
Cooked	Bhat or Bhooja
Parched	Syabaji
Puffed	Golphooki
Uncooked	Chamal
Rosewater	Gulab Jal
Saffron	Kesar
Salt	Nun
Scallion	Hariyo Pyaj
Semolina	Sooji
Sesame Seeds	Til
Soybeans	Bhatmas
Spinach	Palungo
Split Peas	Kerau ko dal
Sweet Potato	Sakarkhanda
Szechwan Pepper or Chinese Peppercorn	Timbur
Tamarind	Amili
Taro, or Eddos	Pindalu
Tea	Chiya
Turmeric	Besar
Turnip	Salgam
Vinegar	Sirkaa
Yam	Tarul
Yogurt	Dahi

THE CONTRIBUTORS

Meena Adhikari
Fried Nepali Crackers, Peas and Tofu Curry, Sweet Yogurt with Spices

Sarita Baidya
Sesame Seed Pickle, Stuffed Bitter Melon, Nepali Egg Bread, Fried Nepali Cookies

Sharda Chopra
Green Mango Chutney, Creamy Onions, Spiced Almond Chicken

Benu Dahal
Potato Pickle, Sun-dried Potato Curry, Crispy Rice Doughnuts, Nepali Doughnuts

Sudha Dhakal
Fried Rice Flakes, Cauliflower and Potato Curry, Egg Curry, Rice Flake Pilaf

Bhuban Dhital
Sun-dried Lentil and Vegetable Balls with Potatoes

Shashi Dhital
Rhubarb Chutney, Dried Vegetable Greens and Soybean Pickle

Beenita Gautam
Tofu, Cauliflower, and Mushroom Stir-fry

Kapila Gautam
Mustard Greens with Rice Flour Sauce, Potatoes and Okra with Soybeans, Grapefruit Salad

Meena Giri
Chicken Cutlets, Fried Puffed Bread, Chickpea-flour Sweets, Mango Ice Cream Cones

Sarojini Gurung
Potato-filled Pastries

Satya Gurung
Hot Potato Curry

Shanti Jonchhe
Rice Pancake, Cauliflower and Green Chili Pickle, Chickpea Curry, Sweet Chickpea Balls, Rice Dumplings with Sesame Seeds and Coconut

Kyoni Joshi
Yellow Lentils, Rice Pudding, Lamb Curry

Indira Karki
Green Chili Pickle, Spicy Whole Potatoes, Spicy Spinach Lentils, Plantain Curry, Mung Bean Fudge

Indira Koirala
Ginger Pickle, Semolina Balls

Bishnu Malakar
Barbecued Pork Spareribs

Indira Malla
Sesame Seed and Spinach Pickle

Rita Nirola
Barbecued Shredded Chicken,
Split Black Lentils

Mukti Pandey
Cucumber and Yogurt Pickle,
Mustard Greens, Spicy Fried Pork
Cubes, Coconut Fudge

Romila Pandey
Lamb or Pork Mo Mo, Mixed
Sprouted Bean Soup

Priti Pant
Mixed Dal, Pan-fried Okra

Sabita Pant
Raisin Pickle, Potato Kabab

Mita Patel
Semolina Pie

Goma Devi Pathak
Gundruk Soup, Pumpkin Vine
Tips, Nepali Corn Bread

Jyoti Pathak
Black Lentil Patties, Hot Spicy
Fish, Nepal Style Quail, Sweet
Yogurt-Pistachio Dessert, Home-
made Yogurt

Ramji Prajapati
Baked Sour Cream Squares

Pratima Rimal
Prawn Curry, Dessert Croissant

Gyanu Shah
Sweet Bread

Bhadrika Sharma
Grilled Tomato and Dried Shrimp
Chutney, Celery and Potato
Pickle, Daikon Radish Pickle,
Onion Pickle, Roasted Sesame
Seed and Cilantro Pickle, Plain
Wheat Flat Bread, Flaky Wheat
Bread, Rice Salad, Cornmeal
Porridge, Wheat-flour Pudding

Carolyn Sharma
Hot Tomato Pickle, Pork Chops
and Rice, Spanish Chicken and
Rice

Indira Sharma
Green Tomato Chutney, Mixed
Vegetable Curry, Rice Flakes with
Nuts and Lentils, Pan-Fried
Asparagus and Potatoes, Chicken
Curry, Plain Rice, Fried Rice with
Peas

Raj Sharma
Elephant-Ear Leaves and Stem
Curry, Lamb Curry with Cauli-
flower and Peas

Renu Sharma
Mixed Vegetable Fritters

Kanti Shimkhada
Potato Roll

Shanta Shukla
Mashed Eggplant Pickle

Bimala Shrestha
Nepali Peda Cookies

Vijaya Shrestha
Bamboo-Shoot Medley, Dessert
Balls in Syrup

Rita Stecklein
Mushroom and Potato Curry,
Pork Curry, Almond Fudge

Puspa Subedi
Turkey Mo Mo, Twice-cooked
Chutney, Tomato and Cilantro
Chutney, Chickpea Curry,
Marinated Lamb Kabob, Ricotta
Cheese Squares in Cream, Carrot
Fudge

Nirakar Thakur
Easy Tomato Pickle,
Fish Curry

Durga Thapa
Fish Pickle

Rita Thapa
Fried Chicken Gizzard, Chicken Fried Rice

Sandhya Rajya Thapa
Lemon Bread, Scalloped Potatoes with Cheese and Herbs

Amrit Tuladhar
Roasted or Grilled Meat, Chicken Drumsticks, Rekha's Sweet Balls

Arun Tuladhar
Potato, Tomato, and Onion Curry; Chicken Chow Chow

Shakuntala Tuladhar
Cabbage Pickle, Cucumber Pickle, Mo Mo, Turkey Turnovers

Pratima Upadhya
Fried Lentil Balls with Yogurt, Tuna-Potato Cutlet

Gunu Upadhyay
Nepali Peda Cookies

Sama Wagle
Roasted Sesame Seeds and Spinach Pickle, Ground Turkey and Mixed Bean Soup

Laden Yoklin
Potato Balls Filled with Meat